The Revolution of Beelzebub

THE REVOLUTION
OF BEELZEBUB

GNOSIS, ANTHROPOGENESIS,
AND THE WAR IN HEAVEN

Samael Aun Weor

THELEMA PRESS
2007

PUBLISHERS NOTE: When seen in this book, the symbol † indicates additional information available in the Glossary on page 163.

The Revolution of Beelzebub
A Thelema Press Book / June 2002
Second Edition (English) 2007

Originally published as "La Revolucion de Beelzebub," 1950.

English Edition © 2007 Thelema Press

ISBN 978-1-934206-18-8

Thelema Press is a non-profit organization delivering to humanity the teachings of Samael Aun Weor. All proceeds go to further the distribution of these books. For more information, visit our website.

www.gnosticteachings.org
www.gnosticradio.org
www.gnosticschool.org
www.gnosticstore.org
www.gnosticvideos.org

Contents

Illustrations

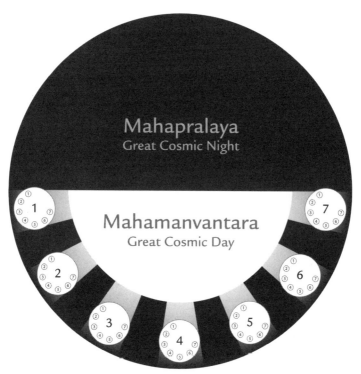

One Mahamanvatara is subdivided into seven
Manvantaras. Further, one Manvantara is
subdivided into seven periods or epochs.

Editor's Introduction

The Seven Cosmic Rounds

All creation manifests in cycles of cosmic days. A cosmic day in Sanskrit is a *Manvantara*. A cosmic night is called a *Pralaya*.

A *Mahamanvantara* is a great cosmic day (*maha* = great). One great cosmic day is equivilent to 311,040,000,000,000 human years. A great cosmic night is called a *Mahapralaya*.

Each Mahamanvantara is a progression of seven Manvantaras. And each Mantavara is a progression of seven periods or epochs. So one Mahamanvantara contains seven manvantaras, and each manvantara contains seven "lesser" manvataras (or ages or periods or epochs). Each of them are a recapitulation of past Manvantaras and an example of future Manvantaras. That is why we can also call these periods or epochs Manvantaras.

In synthesis, "Manvantara" is a cosmic activity of life and a "Pralaya" is a respose of that activity. For instance, now that you are alive, you are in your particular individual human "Manvantara," and when you are physically dead you are in your particular individual human "Pralaya."

From H.P. Blavatsky:

> "The Days of Nights of Brahma. This is the name
> given to the Periods called Manvantara (Manuantara,
> or between the Manus) and Pralaya (Dissolution); one
> referring to the active periods of the Universe, the other
> to its times of relative and complete rest -- according to
> whether they occur at the end of a 'Day,' or an 'Age' (a
> life) of Brahma. These periods, which follow each other
> in regular succession, are also called Kalpas, small and
> great, the minor and the Maha Kalpa; though, properly
> speaking, the Maha Kalpa is never a 'day,' but a whole
> life or age of Brahma, for it is said in the *Brahma Vaivarta*:
> 'Chronologers compute a Kalpa by the Life of Brahma;
> minor Kalpas, as Samvarta and the rest, are numerous.'
> In sober truth they are infinite; as they have never had a

commencement, i.e., there never was a first Kalpa, nor will there ever be a last one, in Eternity."

"Occultism divides the periods of Rest (Pralaya) into several kinds; there is the individual pralaya of each Globe, as humanity and life pass on to the next; seven minor Pralayas in each Round; the planetary Pralaya, when seven Rounds are completed; the Solar Pralaya, when the whole system is at an end; and finally the Universal Maha -- or Brahma -- Pralaya at the close of the 'Age of Brahma.' These are the three chief pralayas or 'destruction periods.' There are many other minor ones, but with these we are not concerned at present."

Aquarian Era

Dedication

I dedicate this book to the human beings with wills of steel, to the great rebels, to the high flying eagles, to those who never humble themselves before the whip of any tyrant, to the supermen of humanity, and also to the great repentant sinners, since from them a new race of gods will be the outcome.

In order to reach the High Initiation one does not need to be erudite. Instead, one needs to be perfect as our Father who is in heaven is perfect.

One does not reach High Initiation with the intellect, but with the heart. Consequently, there are true Masters of the White Fraternity who do not know how to read, nor to write. Nevertheless, they are great illuminated sages.

The intellect never attains Initiation. Only the heart attains the Golgotha of the High Initiation. The majority of people have their heads filled with absurd theories and ancestral prejudices; they do not open their minds to anything new.

Justice is the supreme piety and the supreme impiety of the law.

The Gods judged the Great Whore (humanity), and they considered her unworthy; thus, the sentence of the Gods is:

To the abyss!

To the abyss!

To the abyss!

Human beings of the Aquarian age! Beings of the twenty-first century! Beings of the thirtieth century, remain firm within the light, remember that the human beings of the twentieth century were barbarians, and that all of them were punished because of their evilness. Let this serve as an example, so that you will remain firm within the faith of Christ.

Beings of Aquarius! Exert yourselves on your path towards the light. Redeem and fuse yourselves with your Innermost, before the evil ones of this twentieth century leave the abyss. A new sign of darkness is approaching (Capricorn). Therefore, it is the time for you to be alert and vigilant, because the Earth will again be invaded by the Demon-Souls of this Dark Age, who I, Aun Weor[1], bound into the abyss in order for you to have the happiness that you are now enjoying.

Beings of Aquarius! I especially dedicate to you this book that the barbarians of the twentieth century did not understand. People from this twentieth century heard the word of Jehovah:

> *Thus saith Jehovah of hosts; even so will I break this people and this city, as one breaketh a potter's vessel, that cannot be made whole again: and they shall bury them in Tophet (the killing valley), till there be no place to bury.* - Jeremiah 19: 11

---

1 - Aun Weor is the Inner Being of Samael Aun Weor.

Introduction

Surveying from a height within infinite space, searching and lurking within the Akashic Records of Nature, I could verify for myself that the Moon is the mother of the Earth.

Now, with the open Eye of Dangma,† I will submerge myself within the Great Alaya, the famous super-soul of Emerson, the soul of the Universe. I invite you, beloved reader, to deeply study this book. It is necessary to meditate on it, to go deeply into its content, to know its profound significance.

If you ask me who I, Samael Aun Weor, am, I would answer you that I am one of the seven Amsha-Spentas of the Zoroastrians, who was active in the past Mahamanvantara (cosmic day) that was named the Lotus of Gold.

Therefore, I am going to give testimony of that which I have seen and heard. Listen to me, men and Gods: I know in depth about the seven Mysteries of the Moon, the seven Jewels, the seven Surges of Life which evolved and devolved within that which the Theosophists call the "Lunar Chain."

Certainly, the Moon is the satellite of the Earth only in one sense. What I am referring to is that it rotates around our planet.

When this matter is seen from another angle, when it is investigated with the Eye of Shiva (intense spiritual vision of the Adept or Jivan-Mukta), then truly, the Earth becomes the satellite of the Moon.

The evidence in favor of this fact is found in the tides, in the changing cycles of the many forms of sicknesses which coincide with the lunar phases, in what we can observe within the development of plants, and in the very marked lunar influence within the phenomena of conception and gestation of all creatures.

The Moon was once an inhabited planet, but now it is just cold refuse, a shadow that is dragged by the new body (the Earth), which is where all of its powers and principles of life have been passed by transfusion. It is condemned to be in pursuit of the Earth throughout many ages. The Moon looks like a satellite, but it is a mother which rotates around its daughter (the Earth).

I lived among the Lunar humanity. I knew its seven Root Races, its epochs of civilization and barbarism, its alternating cycles of evolution and involution.

When the Selenites arrived to the sixth sub-race of the Fourth Round (the same age which this Terrestrial humanity has already reached) I accomplished a similar mission to the one which I am accomplishing in these moments on the planet in which we live.

I taught to the people of the Moon the Synthesis-Religion, which is contained within the Initiatic Stone (Sex), the doctrine of Jano (I.A.O.) or the doctrine of the Jinns.

I lit the flame of Gnosis among the Selenites; I formed a Gnostic Movement there. Thus, I sowed the seed... and as I sowed, some seeds fell by the wayside, and the mundane fowls of the air devoured them.

Some seeds fell upon rocks of discussions, theories and anxieties where profound and reflective people did not exist. As soon as they sprung up, they withered away before the light of the sun, for they did not pass the ordeal of fire, as they did not have roots.

Some fell among the thorns of brothers and sisters who hurt each other with their thorns of slander and gossip, etc. So, the thorns sprang up with the seeds and choked them.

Fortunately, my labor as a sower was not in vain, since some seeds fell on good ground, and sprang up, and bore fruit, some a hundredfold, some sixtyfold, some thirtyfold.

Many latent faculties exist within the Devamatri, Aditi or Cosmic Space, inside the Runic UR within the Microcosmos, the "machine-man," or better if we say, the Intellectual Animal†, that could be developed through tremendous, intimate super-efforts.

On the ancient Moon, in the times before it became a corpse, those who accepted the Synthesis-Religion of Jano became saved, and they transformed themselves into Angels. Nevertheless, the great majority, those who were enemies of the Maithuna†, those who rejected the Initiatic Stone (Sex), converted themselves into Lucifers, terribly perverse demons to which the Bible refers.

Usually, a third party is never missing; so, in that Lunar Apocalypse, a certain cold group at last became fiery, and they accepted the work in the Ninth Sphere (Sex). A new abode was granted to these people, in order for them to work with the Brute Stone until giving it perfect cubic form.

> *The stone which the builders disallowed, the same is made the head of the corner, and stone of stumbling, and a rock of offense.*
>
> 1 Peter 2: 7-8

In those times, the Selenites had a dreadful, sanguinary religion. The Pontiffs of that cult sentenced me with the death penalty, and I was crucified upon the summit of a mountain close to a great city.

The transference of all the vital powers of the Moon to this planet Earth left that old Selenite abode without life. Therefore, the Lunar-Soul is now reincarnated in this world upon which we live.

I was absorbed within the Absolute at the end of that Lunar Mahamanvantara, which endured 311,040,000,000,000 years, or, in other words, an age of Brahma.

It is indispensable to say that after the Great Day, the Monadic waves of the Moon submerged themselves within the Runic UR, within the profound womb of the Eternal Mother-Space.

It is urgent to affirm that during such a Maha-Samadhi (Ecstasy without end), we (the Monadic waves) penetrated much more deeply, and thus we arrived to the Father, Brahma, the Universal Spirit of Life.

It is necessary to clarify that Brahma submerged Himself into the Absolute during the whole period of the Maha-Pralaya, the Great Night.

While we, the Brethren, were in that tremendous Para-Nirvanic repose, the Unknown Darkness converted itself into Uncreated Light for us.

UHR is the clock, the measurement of time; thus, the Mahamanvantara RHU is the repose, the Great Pralaya.

Certainly, the Cosmic Night endures as much as the Great Day. It is my duty to affirm that each one of us, the Brethren, was radically absorbed within his own primordial atom, the Ain Soph.

Therefore, when the dawn of this new Cosmic Day was initiated, the Eternal Mother-Space expanded herself from inside towards the outer like a lotus bud. This is how this Universe was gestated inside the womb of Prakriti.

CHAPTER 1

The Revolution of Beelzebub

Sing unto the majesty of fire, oh Goddess of wisdom.

Let us raise our cups and let us toast to the hierarchies of the flames...

Let us ignite our amphoras of gold and let us drink the wine of light until becoming inebriated...

Oh Demosthenes†, how fast were your feet in Cheronea...

Mesmer†, Cagliostro†, Agrippa†, Raymond Lully†, I knew all of you; I saw all of you, and they called you madmen.

From where did you get your wisdom? Why were your lips sealed with death? What happened to your knowledge?

On this night, I will drink the wine of wisdom within the chalice of your august craniums and in a gesture of omnipotent rebellion, I will revolt against the ancient tomb.

I will break all the chains of the world, and I will declare myself immortal even if they believe me to be crazy...

I will grasp the sword of Damocles†, so as to make the inopportune guest to flee....

Thus mute skull, you will not succeed against me, since I am eternal...

Igneous Christ, blazing Christ, I raise my cup and make a toast to the Gods, but you baptize me with fire...

From where did this manifold creation spring?

From where did these immense planetary boulders spring that seem to emerge as millenarian monsters from the faucet of an abyss in order to fall into yet another abyss more terrible and dreadful than the first?

I lift my eyes up high, and upon the igneous head of the most exalted among all the sacrificed ones, I read this word: **I.N.R.I.**

IGNIS NATURA RENOVATUR INTEGRA.
Fire renews nature incessantly.

Elijah taken up to Heaven in a Chariot of Fire.

Engraving by Gustave Doré

Yes, beloved disciples, the entire universe is nothing else but the granulations of the Fohat (fire).

Oh, the hierarchies of the fires! Oh, the hierarchies of the flames.

Ardent, ardent roses... igneous serpents... hiss... hiss eternally upon the waters of life in order for the worlds to emerge...

Hiss, hiss, hiss eternally with the hiss of the Fohat, oh holy flames...

Blessed be the luminous fiat, the spermatic fiat of the eternal living God, who placed this universe into existence.

Divine fire, you are the divine numen of all infinite existences, and when the subterranean flame bursts its prison and devours the framework... burning the foundations of the world, you shall still be as you were before, without suffering any change. Oh, divine and eternal fire!....

The Fohat fecundates the chaotic matter; thus, the worlds emerge into existence. All of what has been, what is, and what will be, is a child of fire...

The fire of the Holy Spirit is the flame of Horeb... The Fohat lives within our testicles (ovaries) and it is only a matter of putting it into activity, by means of Sexual Magic, to convert ourselves into Gods... into Devas, into divine and ineffable beings.

The fire of chastity is the fire of the Holy Spirit, it is the fire of Pentecost, it is the fire of Kundalini... It is the fire which Prometheus† plundered from heaven... It is the sacred flame of the temple, ignited by the vestals†... It is the flame of triple incandescence... It is the chariot of fire on which Elijah ascended into heaven.

In the time of ancient Egypt, the neophyte who aspired to become an Alchemist had to wed a mature woman in order to awaken the divine fire. But, if he married a young maiden, he had to wait some months before executing the sexual connection. Obedience to his wife was one of the matrimonial requirements, to which the Alchemist submitted with great gladness.

To introduce the virile member into the feminine vagina and to withdraw it without spilling the semen is the old formula of ancient alchemists... This is the formula to awaken the igneous serpent and to achieve union with the Innermost. According to Moses, the Innermost is the Real Being, the Ruach Elohim, who sowed the waters in the beginning of the world.

This is how we convert ourselves into the Sun King, into the Triumphant Magi of the Snake... We become omnipotent Gods, and with the sword of Damocles, we defeat death... All of Nature kneels before us, and the tempests serve as carpets for our feet.

Fohat is the Elixir of Long Life. We can preserve the body for millions of years with this elixir...

The woman is the vestal of the temple... the woman lights the flame of our sounding arquin, which vibrates within the cosmic spaces with the tremendous solemn and ineffable euphoria of the vast heavens of Urania†...

Woman, I love Thee...
It has been many nights
that I weep dearly...dearly...
but at the end of the journey I hear thy songs,
and the dreaming stars tremble with love.
Then, the celestial muses kiss themselves with thy
    chants...
Thou art a sealed book of seven seals.
I do not know if Thou art joy or venom.
I am at the edge of an abyss which I do not
    understand:
I feel fear of Thee and of thy mystery.
Woman, I adore Thee...

I want to drink the mandrake's liquor,
I want to kiss thy bosom,
I want to feel the chant of thy words
and I want to ignite my fires.

Woman, Thou cannot forget me,
Thou told me that Thou loves me
and Thou swore to me thy love,
in those adored nights...
in those nights of idyll...
in those perfumed nights...
nights of chants and nests...

Ancient Priestess, ignite my wick,
ignite my flame of triple incandescence;
nubile Vestal of a divine temple...
deliver to me the fruits of science...

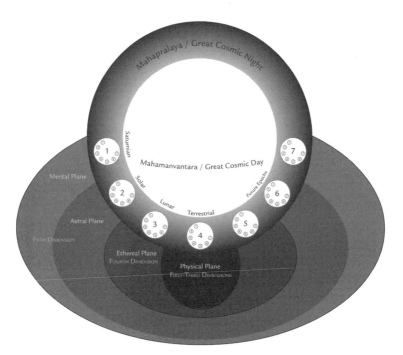

The Saturnian Epoch was developed within the parallel universe of the fifth dimension, specifically in the mental plane.

CHAPTER 2

Arcadia

Who is that young man with a greyish tunic, black and profound eyes, hawk-nose, tall body, and tousled mane?

Who is that joyful young man who laughs happily while in social gatherings with friends, who is broad-minded and blissful in an orgy?

Ah! He is Beelzebub, the king of parties, the simpatico friend of taverns, the joyful friend of orgies, the romantic, handsome, broad-minded man from ancient Arcadia...

I have clairvoyantly penetrated into the epoch of Saturn... I do not see anything vague or vaporous here, as Besant†, Leadbeater†, Heindel†, and Steiner† asserted. What of their powers? What of their knowledge? Why did they speak to me of vague things when everything that I see here is concrete and exact?

These human beings of the epoch of Saturn were Human... true Humans†, because they had a Being, and they knew that this Being was within them...

Humanities are always analogous, and these human beings of the epoch of Saturn were like the present human beings with a similar environment.

When speaking of humanity, what may come into our minds is business, taverns, brothels, orgies, beautiful, frivolous maidens and handsome suitors, abducted princesses and ancient castles, neighboring sweethearts and nighthawk poets, an elder who passes by and a child who cries, a mother who sings a lullaby of hope, or a monk who murmurs a prayer... To that end, the whole gamut of qualities, the various and diverse defects, are what constitute the human values...

Humanity is a womb where angels and demons are gestated. Therefore, the only outcome of humanity is nothing else but angels and demons...

There is no danger when the divine Monads† animate the three inferior kingdoms.[1] Danger exists when they arrive at the human

---

1 - The mineral, plant, and animal kingdoms in ascending order.

kingdom, because from this human state an angel or a demon is the only outcome...

Beelzebub was a great rebel who shook his head and his tousled mane amidst the cups and delights of Arcadia... He had longings for wisdom, but his rebel eagle wings did not fit among the parochial rabble. His tremendous and fierce word, with its magnificent and luminous proverbs, disturbed the imbeciles and unmasked the traitors...

The fire of eternity was burning within his soul and a scream of rebellion was shaking his titanic innermost parts; yet, he was enjoying all kinds of commodities and he was abiding in a comfortable and luxurious house of Arcadia, which was his rebel eagle's nest...

All was of a mental matter; all of the human beings used Astral bodies... They ate, dressed, drank and enjoyed themselves like in this present time, because the Astral Body is an organism almost as dense as the physical. Thus, it was analogously constituted as the physical body...

Certainly, these human beings of Arcadia were remembering ancient cataclysms and beautiful millenarian traditions from pre-saturnine epochs... but within the complete apogee of the human state, life was similar to that of the present time...

Small, festive parties...
of happy comrades...
pale fires...
and liquors of mandrake.

Nights of revelry and orgy...
nights of carnival...
Romances of love and poetry...
that are better not to remember...

Chaste brunette maidens
who fall upon the arms...
and who are weightless as the wind
with those raiments of satin...

The Guardian of the Threshold is our Satan... our internal beast, the
source of all of our animal passions and brutal appetites...

Engraving by Gustave Doré

CHAPTER 3
White Magic and Black Magic

There are seven truths, seven sublime lords, and seven secrets...

The secret of the abyss is one of the seven great unutterable secrets...

Abbadon is the angel of the abyss. He wears a black tunic and a red cap, like those worn by the Drukpas† and Bons†1 from oriental Tibet and from the regions of Sikkim and Bhutan, also as worn by the black magicians from the altar of Mathra (pronounced "Mazra" by the Rosicrucian school A.M.O.R.C.† from California).

The venerable Anagarikas† are also red cap magicians. To that end, all of these black magicians are the great hierarchies from the tenebrous caverns...

Theurgy is one thing and Necromancy is another... The internal master of the Theurgist is the Innermost†. The internal master of the Necromancer is his Guardian of the Threshold whom they call the guardian of their consciousness, the guardian of the precinct, the guardian of their chamber, the guardian of their sanctum...

The Innermost is our Divine Spirit, our Real Being, our Internal Angel.

The Guardian of the Threshold is the internal depth of our animal "I."

The Innermost is the ardent flame of Horeb. In accordance with Moses, the Innermost is the Ruach Elohim who sowed the waters in the beginning of the world. He is the Sun King, our Divine Monad, the Alter-Ego of Cicerone.

The Guardian of the Threshold is our Satan... our internal beast, the source of all of our animal passions and brutal appetites...

The Real Being of the Theurgist is the Innermost. The superior "I" of the Necromancer is the Guardian of the Threshold.

The powers of the Innermost are divine. The powers of the Guardian of the Threshold are diabolic.

---

1 - The author later clarified that the Bons are not all black. See the glossary.

The Theurgist worships the Innermost. The Necromancer worships the Guardian of the Threshold.

The Theurgist avails himself with the power of his Innermost in order to perform his great works of practical magic. The Necromancer worships the Guardian of the Threshold for his works of black magic.

We have arrived at the omnipotent empire of high and low magic.

The Astral Light is the battle field between white and black magicians. The Astral Light is the clue of all empires and the key of all powers. It is the great universal agent of life. All the columns of angels and demons live within the Astral Light...

In order to attain Theurgy one firstly needs to be an Alchemist, and it is impossible to be an Alchemist without a spouse.

"**V.I.T.R.I.O.L.**" is one of the clues of the Gnostic Alchemist. The word signifies:

> VISITAM INTERIOREM TERRE
> RECTIFICATUM INVENIAS
> OCULTUM LAPIDUM.
>
> *Visit the interior of the earth,*
> *which through rectifying you*
> *will find the occult stone.*

The clue is found within the flexible and malleable liquid glass... This liquid glass is the semen. Therefore, we have to sink ourselves within our own organic laboratory to increase, to rectify, our liquid glass, with the goal of heroically expanding the philosophical stone, the force of Nous, the Immortal Logos†, the Solar Snake, which sleeps with silent inquietude within the bottom of our ark.

The woman is the vestal of the temple. The vestal is the one who ignites the sacred fire of triple incandescence.

The Elixir of Long Life is the potable gold, and that potable gold is the semen... The secret is to sexually connect oneself with the priestess-wife and withdraw from her without spilling the semen.

I A O: These three vowels must be pronounced[1] during the sexual trance as follows:

Iiiiiiiiiiiiiiiiiiii Aaaaaaaaaaaaa Oooooooooooooo

Each letter requires a complete inhalation into our lungs. One completely fills his lungs and vocalizes the first vowel; one then completely fills his lungs again and pronounces the second vowel, and likewise the third.

This must be performed mentally in cases when the spouse is not prepared, in order to avoid wrong interpretations on their behalf.

The Kundalini awakens with this clue. We finally attain the marriage of Nous, and we conquer the beautiful Helen, the one for whom all the illustrious warriors of ancient Troy fought.

The beautiful Helen is the igneous mind of the soul who is already betrothed to her eternal beloved, to her Innermost.

The beautiful Helen is the ardent mind of the Theurgist. The Theurgist transmutes the lead into real and permanent gold... The Theurgist grasps the sword and as a King of Nature he resurrects the dead, heals the blind, the crippled and paralytics... He unleashes the hurricanes and heroically walks through the fiery gardens of Nature.

What inductive or deductive logic serves as a foundation for the Neoplatonic Plotinus† and Porphirius† in order to combat the phenomenon of Theurgy?

All of the infinite existences of the universe are children of the phenomenon of Theurgy... There exists an enormous difference between the mirror of Theurgy and the mirror of Necromancy. The mirror of Eleusis† is different from the mirror of Sodom†.

The mirror of the school of Sodom is Necromancy and black magic. The mirror of the mysteries of Eleusis is pure and divine Theurgy.

The Initiate of Eleusis, while in the state of *Manteia* (ecstasy), pronounced the sacred syllable. Then, the Initiate's Innermost appeared with light and beauty within the resplendent mirror... Many times the Initiate provoked the state of Manteia when

---

1 - These vowels are pronounced as: I as in "tree," A as in "tall," O as in "low."

drinking from the chalice of Soma.† He was thus transported into the ineffable pleroma† of love.

The Necromancer of the school of Sodom begs the Guardian of the Threshold to appear in the mirror. Once the vision appears, the candidate becomes a slave of the Guardian of the Threshold and is converted into a black magician.

The ritual of first degree of the school of Sodom is the most monstrous crime ever committed against humanity. While staring in the mirror, the disciple invokes the monster of the threshold with these following questions that he asks himself:

1) Do you want to know the mystery of your being?

2) Would you like to know the terror of the threshold?

3) Would you listen to the voice that answers?

4) Did you ever hear the consciousness?

5) Do you know that the consciousness is the internal voice that speaks when it has an opportunity to do so?

6) Would you give the consciousness the freedom of speaking to you?

7) Do you know that the consciousness is your guardian and therefore the guardian of this Sanctum?

8) And do you know that this sacred guardian will always be present in this sanctum in order to guide you and protect you?

These questions are asked by the naive disciple, and after reciting some other paragraphs of black magic before the mirror, he says:

"Before my brethren and lords and in the presence of the guardian of the Sanctum, I declare that I have approached the terror of the Threshold and that I do not have terror for my soul. Now I am a dweller of the threshold; I have been purified and I have commanded my true "I" (the Guardian of the Threshold) to exercise dominion over my physical body and mind."

This is how the naive disciple is converted into a black magician, into a slave of the Guardian of the Threshold and of the darkness.

This ritual of black magic, adapted for this XX century, is very ancient. Beelzebub started his horrible career as a demon after having performed it in ancient Arcadia. In 1387, with just reason, the Tibetan reformer Tsong Khapa† cast every book of Necromancy that he found into flames. As a result, some discontent Lamas formed an alliance with the aboriginal Bons, and today they form a powerful sect of black magic in the regions of Sikkim, Bhutan and Nepal, submitting themselves to the most abominable black rites.

Iamblichus†, the great Theurgist, said:

> Theurgy unites us more strongly with divine nature. This nature is engendered by itself and acts in accordance with its own powers. It is intelligent and sustains everything; it is the ornament of the universe and invites us to the intelligent truth, to perfection, and to share this perfection with others. It unites us so intimately to all the creative acts of the Gods in proportion to the capacity of each one of us. After accomplishing these sacred rites, the soul is consolidated within the actions of the intelligence of the Gods until identifying itself with them. Thus it is absorbed by the primeval and divine Essence. Such is the object of the sacred initiations of the Egyptians.

Iamblichus was invoking and materializing the planetary gods.

Firstly, one becomes an Alchemist, then a Magician, and finally a Theurgist. We awaken the snake and become Theurgists by practicing Sexual Magic. The whole secret resides in learning how to sexually connect ourselves with our spouse and to withdraw without spilling the semen (without reaching the orgasm).

Naked dances, Sexual Magic, and delectable music were something ineffable in the mysteries of Eleusis.

The Gnostic Church has opened its doors to all of humanity, and the mission of diffusing the snake's wisdom unto this suffering humanity has been granted to me, Samael Aun Weor.

Eleusis

Manteia, Manteia, Manteia...†
The music of the temple inebriates me
With this delectable chant...
And this sacred dance.

And the exotic priestesses dance
with the impetuous frenzy of fire
distributing light and smiles,
in that corner of paradise.

Manteia, Manteia, Manteia,
and the serpent of fire,
amongst the august marble,
is the princess of the sacred purple,
it is the virgin of very ancient castles.

It is Hadit, the winged serpent,
engraved on the ancient roads of granite,
like a terrific and adored Goddess,
like a genie of an ancient monolith,
in the body of the Gods entwined.

And I saw in festival nights,
delectable princesses on their berths,
and the silent muse was smiling on the altars
among the perfumes and silk.

Manteia, Manteia, Manteia,
shouted the vestals,
filled with a crazy, divine frenzy,
and silently looking at them were the gods immortal,
under the porches of alabaster.

Kiss me, my love, look at me, I love you...
And a whisper of delectable words
was shaking the sacred arcanum...
among the music and roses
of that sacred sanctuary.

Go dance exotic dancers of Eleusis
among the jingle of your tiny bells,
Magdalenes of a Via Crucis,
divine priestesses...

♀ ♉   Indecision   ך 6

The human being is found between vice and virtue, the Virgin
and the Whore, Urania-Venus and the Medusa... Arcanum
number six is the struggle between the Spirit and the bestial,
between God and the devil...

FROM TAROT AND KABBALAH BY SAMAEL AUN WEOR

CHAPTER 4

The Two Ways

Behold, I set before you the way of life and the way of death.
Jeremiah 21:8

The bewitching flower of crime grows in the shadow of liquor and the orgy.

The wild vermin and the writhing reptile make their nest by the shadow of the nubile foliage of passion.

In the middle of all the revelry and the bacchanalia, Beelzebub learned to gamble with a great amount of money. In reality, money and the original sin are coexistential: both are the tragedy of the human.

Gambling has driven the elegant lady and the cunning gentleman, as well as the working man and the bohemian gambler, to ruin and suicide.

Beelzebub learned the vice of gambling, and he laughed happily while in the bacchanalia amidst the bare sound of the dice and the happy and triumphant pop of another bottle.

Yet, lo and behold, a mysterious personage was never absent within the orgy. This ominous personage with a sinister face wore a black tunic of Arcadian style and great rings of gold were always shining in his ears.

What mystery was surrounding this sinister personage?

Was he perhaps a genie of the light who came from remote spheres?

Was he perhaps some luminous lord of the flame or some ancient inhabitant from some historical epoch already ended?

No, nothing of the sort. This man was only a horrible and monstrous transgressor of the law, a black magician.

Beelzebub learned certain clues from this black magician in order to win in the vice of gambling. Their friendship was mingled with thankfulness and orgies. Thus, this sinister personage was conducing his victim along the black path...

The human beings of the epoch of Saturn were using Astral bodies and they were tall in stature. At that time, our modern human bodies were only germs with the possibility of unfolding.

The present human "Innermosts" (Spirits) were just virginal sparks who were animating the mineral kingdom. But, Beelzebub was a human being of that epoch because he had a Being and he knew that this Being was within him.

If Beelzebub would have followed the narrow and straight way which leads towards the light, he then would have become a lord of the mind, a son of the fire, like his most beloved friends. However, liquor, pleasure, gambling, and fornication with its exotic flowers of malignant and seductive beauty hypnotize the weak and take them into the abyss.

This is how Beelzebub became an intimate friend of this sinister personage, who with his miraculous clues, was leading him triumphantly in the vice of gambling. Sadly enough, one day Beelzebub was finally prepared in order to receive the first initiation of black magic within a tenebrous temple... His master had made ineffable promises to him. He spoke to him a great deal about love and justice; therefore doubting him was impossible, especially when he was always guiding him triumphantly with his marvelous secrets in the vice of gambling.

Likewise, in this day and age, how can the students of the school of Sodom doubt the Imperator of their sacred order or their "Holy Rituals?" The one who is going to fall does not see the gap.

The ritual of the first tenebrous initiation that the disciple Beelzebub received in the temple is the same first ritual that the students of A.M.O.R.C. perform today in their room in order to receive their first degree. Thus, in the same way that the student of the first degree from "Sodom" remains enslaved by the Guardian of the Threshold after the rite, as well Beelzebub remained enslaved by the Guardian of the Threshold. This is how he started his career as a demon...

What happens is that during the ordinary hours of sleep "Veritas," the Black Guru, takes the disciples of the first black degree in the Astral Body and submits them to a very curious rite which we will now observe:

The disciple goes sporadically around a table a few times; he strikes it; then he receives a brick from the hands of the initiator, who ceremoniously pronounces these words: "Underneath the devil, do not forget it." Afterwards, the disciple buries the brick under the ground.

This ceremony symbolizes that the poor disciple has laid the foundation for his black fellowship and that he now has to obey the commands of the black fraternity. Afterwards, certain occult treatments are made upon the principal chakras of the head of this naive victim with the goal of controlling him for the service of the black brotherhood. Also, a lens in the form of an eye is placed upon his neck in order to have influence over the important centers of his subconsciousness. When the disciple awakens upon his bed, he does not bring back any memory of what happened in the Astral plane.

The black magicians have their mysticism, and they always firmly believe that they walk on the good path. No black magician believes that he walks on the evil path.

The path of black magic is a broad way filled with vices and pleasures.

Mariela, the great female black magician, was filled with a delectable and fatal beauty. With her enchanting voice and tender face, she was agilely and weightlessly slithering upon the soft, thick carpets of the great and splendid halls of the oldest aristocratic lineage of the European nobility. Her seductive voice resounded in the party like a poem of love, like a kiss from the shadows, like ineffable music. She was something like the romance of a symphony of Beethoven. She was Mariela, the great black magician, the splendid lady of all the European courts.

The "seventy souls of the cauldron," with their grey hair, were resembling something like a garden of white daisies among perfume, silk, and the swallow-tailed coats of the royal palaces... They were the seventy souls of the cauldron, a garden of white flowers which were blown by a breath of death.

The testament of the seventy Hellenes was a testament of darkness and death. What about you Angela? That royal vesture with a long gown makes you look like the longed-for fiancee of a lover who never arrives. You look like a mysterious nymph of a delectable enchanted labyrinth; you look like an unforgettable beauty within the velvety night strewn with stars.

How many times I saw you, oh Angela, like a fatal goddess amongst the bewitched mirrors of that elegant hall of witchcraft, where you were a queen of evil. What is the name, oh children of evil, of that splendid mansion which is similar to an idyll?

Ah! It is Javhesemo, the delectable hall of purple and silk. Only fatal love and the beauty of the abyss of evil reign there, and every maiden is a poem, every smile an idyll, and every dance a romance of an unforgettable love... The limber and delicate waist of every malignant beauty is a dancer within the silhouette of a mysterious landscape.

Andrameleck, the wealthy and pompous black magician of China, says that the human being is an angel; therefore, he does not need to suffer. He always advises his friends to enter into the aristocracy, to dress like princes and to collect a lot of money.

The black K.H. when talking about social matters, says that his disciples must be triumphant, and that the disciple who is not triumphant cannot be his disciple.

The black magicians love fornication, and in order to justify themselves, they say such is a divine relationship.

The black magicians greatly know that the souls who move away from their Innermosts eventually disintegrate themselves into the abyss. This is why a spokesman from the teachings of the brothers of the tenebrous caverns says that the soul is just a vesture and that it must be disintegrated, because they only have interest in their "Real Being" and that they long for the construction of their hiding place in the absolute. This is the dangerous mysticism of black magic.

Any neophyte in occult science will easily fall into this philosophy of a terribly malignant and seductive beauty...

The black magicians hate the Christ... and they consider him an evil personage. They say that the Lord Christ was not an Initiate, because no Initiate allows himself to be killed... With this philosophy of darkness the black magicians elaborate their mysticism, and filled with rejoicing, they drink, cohabit, and enjoy themselves... They assist in their great festivities and delectably

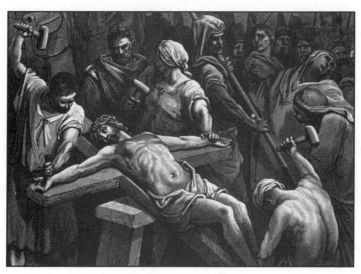

Nailing Christ to the Cross
ENGRAVING BY GUSTAVE DORÉ

dance in their elegant halls while enjoying and laughing in the arms of fornication...

The black path is easy and open. So, Beelzebub, the handsome and simpatico gallant of ancient Arcadia was oriented in this easy and happy path...

> ...*Strait is the gate, and narrow is the way, which leadeth unto light, and few there be that find it (the path which leads unto light is filled with caltrops and thorns). Many are called and few are chosen.*   Matthew 7:13

Therefore, the majority of souls in our terrestrial evolution are lost. The black path, filled with vices and pleasures, was the easier and more accessible path for all of them.

The human evolution has failed! Only a handful of souls will be united with their Innermost and will enter into the angelic kingdom.

The majority of human souls will disintegrate themselves into the abyss throughout the centuries and aeons within the exterior darkness and the weeping and gnashing of teeth.

Christ, the divine Redeemer of the world, came in order to publicly open the Initiatic path for all of humanity.

The whole Via Crucis of the divine Rabbi of Galilee is the path of Initiation that the Initiate must walk on to go towards the Golgotha of High Initiation. Once there, the soul is united with its Innermost and immortalizes itself and reaches the ineffable souls of pleroma.

The lethargy of impenetrable centuries weigh upon the august and sacred mysteries. The Word made flesh lies in the bottom of our sacred ark awaiting the supreme moment of our resurrection.

The holy doctrine of the Savior of the world shines with the luminous and spermatic Fiat of the first instant, and the Rod of Aaron remains waiting for the footsteps of the snake.

The holy Gnostic Church is the zealous guardian of *Pistis Sophia*, the book in which all of the teachings of the Divine Rabbi of Galilee are found written. The very ancient and painful path through which all of the Masters of humanity have walked shines with resplendence in the bottom of all ages.

CHAPTER 5
The Staff of the Patriarchs

Beelzebub, each time more anxious for wisdom, was faithfully and sincerely accomplishing all of the commands which his sinister instructor gave to him.

He knew the course of his seminal currents, and he awoke his Kundalini negatively through the procedures of fornication and concentration, as taught by Necromancy.

The twilight of the cosmic night extended the velvet of its mysterious wings over the profound valleys and over the enormous and gigantic mountains of ancient Arcadia. The corpulent, millenarian trees, the last offspring from unknown parents, had already seen their autumn leaves falling during many long years, but now they seemed to definitively wither in order to fall into the arms of death.

Our current human bodies in those times resembled human phantoms, and the Innermosts of our present humanity had already received their more fine vesture.

Terrible earthquakes shook Arcadia and everywhere a breath of death was sensed. From the enormous multitude of human beings, two types of creatures were the outcome: Angels and demons.

The ancient beauty of Beelzebub, the handsome gallant of Arcadia, had disappeared. His body was covered with hair and he took on the resemblance of a gorilla. His eyes took on the criminal and horrible aspect of a bull. His mouth became gigantic and, with its horrible teeth, presented as the snout of a voracious beast. His head with its enormous mane and his deformed and gigantic feet and hands gave him the aspect of a horrible, corpulent, and enigmatic monster. This was Beelzebub, the enigmatic and handsome gallant of ancient Arcadia...

Was this the cup of wisdom from which he had wanted to drink?

In order to reach such horrible monstrosity, did he have to pass all of those sacred initiations in the temple? Was this the nectar of science or the liquor of wisdom for which he was longing?

Wisdom, divine treasure,
Thou burns me with thy fire,
when I want to cry, I do not,
and if I do, Thou consoles me.

> *There was an old woodsman of the country,*
> *who did not know how to read nor write.*
> *He only loved the edge of his ax;*
> *yet, he felt a longing for life.*

He was watering the furrows with his tears,
while feeling love for Wisdom.
His pale cheeks were smiling
when he inebriated himself with love and poetry.

> *Wisdom, Wisdom, Wisdom,*
> *how much thou burns me*
> *exclaimed the agonizing elder*
> *under the blonde stars.*

Wisdom, liquor of Gods,
is a liquor which poisons,
thus, in a very hard way my spirit will come:
Terrible, oh God of mine, is this torture of waiting.

> *Wisdom, for thee, I raise my cup,*
> *since I am tired of crying.*
> *Wisdom, to thee I chant my strophes*
> *and await within the roses,*
> *the love that must come.*

Wisdom, divine treasure,
Thou burns me with thy fire,
when I want to cry, I do not,
and if I do, Thou consoles me.

Thus, the Kundalini awakened in a negative way and converted Beelzebub into a tenebrous potency of nature.

During passionate fornication, the black magicians take advantage of the moment of seminal ejaculation by means of mental concentration. This is done in order to exert the ascension of the vitalizing hormones, that are segregated by the sexual glands, towards the head. Then, with their mind, they take the hormones into the heart, which then sends them towards the big toe of the right foot. This is how they awaken their Kundalini in a negative way, and convert themselves into the monster with seven heads to which the Book of Revelation (Apocalypse) refers.

There exist schools of black yoga in India which instruct their disciples in that tenebrous science. We can reduce all of the profound studies of occultism into one synthesis: the Serpent. If we spill the semen (reach the orgasm), then we convert ourselves into devils, and if we do not spill it, we convert ourselves into angels.

If the serpent ascends, then we are Gods, but if the serpent descends, then the tail of the Demon is formed in us, and we become demons.

The tail of the Demon (the Kundabuffer) is a prolongation of the Astral counterpart of the coccyx and is the result of the movement of the serpent, downwards, towards the earth.

The Kundalini is the Staff of the Patriarchs, the Rod of Aaron, the Reed of Brahma and the Scepter of the Gods.

The Gnostic Alchemist awakens the Kundalini through the practicing of Sexual Magic. Thus, the Kundalini ascends through a conduit, which is in a canal called Sushumna. This igneous serpent is thick in those who have accumulated a lot of christonic substance (semen), but it is thin in those who have not stored a lot of sexual energy.

The positive awakening of the Kundalini is accompanied by a great festivity within the temple. Terrible pain is produced in the coccyx. Afterwards, the serpentine fire opens its way upwards, towards the head. The passing from one canyon into another is performed in accordance with the moral merits of the disciple. These canyons are the vertebrae of the spinal column; they are also called pyramids.

Any unworthy action takes the Kundalini of that disciple out from one or more canyons, in accordance with the magnitude of the fault. There are 33 canyons that we must conquer in order to reach the High Initiation, that is, the union with the Innermost.

These 33 canyons belong to the 33rd degree of Masonry. They relate also to the 33 years of the life of Christ. Thus, the 33rd degree is only acquired by the Masters of Major Mysteries.

The two 3's when united are the symbol of the union of the matter with the Spirit, the perfect circle of eternity whose center is everywhere and whose circumference is nowhere.

The High Initiation is performed when the Kundalini has already reached the head, but in order for the Kundalini to triumphantly rise through the 33 canyons, it is necessary to practice in detail all of the teachings of the holy Gospels. In order to reach the High Initiation, we must first pass the nine arcades, that is to say, the nine Initiations of Minor Mysteries.

All of the powers of the human being are awakened according to the ascension of the serpentine fire through the spinal column, since each canyon has its occult name and is related with specific powers.

A certain Master of Major Mysteries said that before reaching the High Initiation, he had the weakness of falling into a certain fault; therefore, his Kundalini descended four canyons. Consequently, in order to reconquer them again, he had to struggle very much.

The ordeals of Initiation are extremely severe. The disciple has to follow a perfect, holy and chaste path. Thus, when reaching the Innermost, the human being becomes converted into a Master of Major Mysteries and into a Theurgist.

CHAPTER 6

I Accuse

After a period of cosmic repose, before the start of the Solar epoch, life recapitulated the Saturnian epoch. Then afterwards, the Solar epoch began.

The Earth was shining with resplendence with the ineffable colors of the Astral Light, and the matter of the universe was the same Astral Light.

The physical bodies of our present humanity were developed a little more and these bodies received the Vital body, which in the present time serves as a foundation for the whole human biology.

The angels and demons of the Saturnine epoch floated in the environment of the Solar epoch...

Here we clairvoyantly see Beelzebub, the prince of demons, surrendered to the worst crimes, an active member of a great temple of black magic. He was intensely struggling in order to make proselytes among that humanity of the Solar epoch. Consequently, there were many souls whom he conquered for his tenebrous temple.

Beelzebub descended the thirteen steps of black magic, thus achieving the 13th black initiation, which converted him into a prince of demons. He wore around his waist the sinister cord of seven knots, which is worn by adepts of black magic.

He became skillful in mind control and received the lost word of the black magicians which is written "Mathrem" and which they pronounce "Mazrem." He placed upon his head of long hair the cap of black magic, and covered his wide and hairy shoulders with the black cape of the prince of demons. Upon his forehead appeared the horns of the devil (these horns are the mark of the beast). He became familiar with all the passwords and converted himself into a great hierarch of the Black Lodge, a left hand adept.

The black magicians have some very curious passwords in order to recognize each other: "Arco" is the password for those of second degree. "Kheira" is the word for those of third degree, which they pronounce "Que-I-raa." "Mathra" is the password for those of fourth degree, which they pronounce "Mazra" and which is the lost word for the black magicians.

Mathra is the name of a temple of black magic. This temple is situated in the Jinn state over the Mountain of Pico, or Pico's Mountain, on the Azores Islands.

The black magicians from the altar of Mathra are magicians of the red cap, as are the Bons and Drukpas from Tibet. The black rituals of this day and age come from this tenebrous Atlantean temple and not from Egypt as they falsely claim.

I, Aun Weor, the very ancient Hierophant of Egyptian Mysteries, accuse the Black Lodge before the verdict of the public consciousness of the crime of fraudulence. I accuse this black institution of the crime of attributing to us, the ancient Egyptians, the rituals of black magic, which we never used in Egypt.

I accuse the Black Lodge of the crime of profanation; I accuse the Black Lodge of making merchandise of the souls of men. I accuse the Black Lodge before the verdict of the public consciousness of the horrendous fraud of making their naive disciples believe their institution to be white.

People of America, rise as a single individual in order to once and for all end those dens of corruption which are leading millions of souls into the abyss. Brave people, heroic people, the hour of the great revolution has arrived, and there is no time to waste.

The hour of great decisions has arrived, and we, all human beings, must reunite ourselves around the Divine Rabbi of Galilee, who from the summits of Golgotha exclaims:

My Lord, My Lord how hast thou glorified me!

The black magicians of the fifth degree will scream their password "Astro" in vain, because that den of black magic will sink into the abyss, where the great beast and the false prophet abide.

The horrible victims of the sixth degree will scream "Zocas, Zocas, Zocas" in vain, because the edge of the sword of cosmic justice will seal their throats within the horrible darkness of desperation, where only weeping and the gnashing of teeth are heard.

What about you, black mystics of the seventh degree? In vain will you burn the witches' salt with alcohol and incense. The filthy guardian of your sanctum will be incapable of saving you from the darkness and desperation, because the millennium has arrived, and all of them who are not near to Christ will go into the abyss, even if they scream "Mathrem, Mathrem, Mathrem" as madmen.

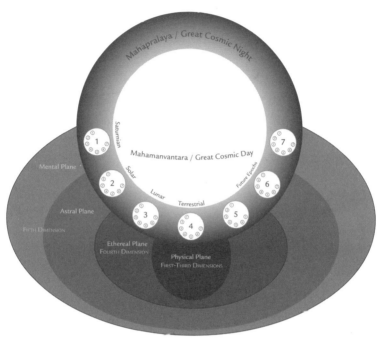

The Solar Epoch was developed within the parallel universe of the
fifth dimension, specifically in the astral plane.

CHAPTER 7

The Atom Nous
The Solar Period

Beelzebub, the prince of demons, was expanding the lines of his legions with new proselytes which he daily recruited among the human beings of the Solar epoch. In this way he converted himself into a hierarch of legions.

Filled with an ineffable beauty, the universe was resplendently shining. The humanity from the Solar epoch was similar to the humanities of any epoch. There was one among the human beings of that epoch who was tremendously struggling in order to attain perfection. This man was later known as Christ, the Divine Rabbi of Galilee, the Solar Logos.

There was another temple of black magic in the Solar epoch in which many human beings were initiated. They were later converted into demons. Astaroth was initiated in that black and gigantic temple.

When the cosmic night of the Solar epoch approached, after millions of years, the Four Lords of Flame endowed the present human Innermosts (Spirits) with a Spiritual Soul or Buddhic body, which is the body of intuition.

The vehicle of intuition is directly connected with the heart. Accordingly, the heart is the center of intuition. Its chakra or lotus flower spins and shines with extraordinary beauty. Seven atomic centers exist in this chakra, which serve as instruments for the Seven Great Cosmic Hierarchies, in order for them to act upon our marvelous organism.

As we have already stated in our book entitled *The Perfect Matrimony or The Door to Enter into Initiation,* the heart of the Sun is constructed like the heart of our human organism. Just as Seven Hierarchs exist in the Sun, who direct the seven cosmic rays, seven brains exist in our heart which belong to the Seven Great Cosmic Hierarchies.

The Sun has an atomic central nucleus, which is the Atom Nous, and this atom is the dwelling of Brahma within us. This atom is the first vital center which functions in the fetus and also the last atom which stops living in our organism.

This atom contains the mind, life, energy, and willpower of the human being. It has an opal-like luminous aura which irradiates and shines.

At the end of the Solar epoch, the humanity of that epoch attained the Angelic state. They are the Archangels of present times. The highest initiate among them was Christ. But not all of the human beings of that epoch reached that state, since the majority converted themselves into demons.

Javhe is the contrary pole of Christ. Javhe was the highest black and tenebrous Initiate of that epoch. When the Cosmic Night arrived, then the universe seemed to submerge itself into the Chaos. All of Nature entered into a happy dream... The seeds of all living things delivered themselves into the arms of dreams... Thus, the harps of the Elohim were delectably vibrating within the infinite spaces.

CHAPTER 8
The Mind and Intuition

The intellectual man lives in his head with its seven portals. The brain is made in order to elaborate thought, yet it is not thought. The brain is nothing but an instrument of the Mental Body.

The Mental Body is a material organism, yet it is not the physical organism. The Mental Body has its ultra-biology and its internal pathology, which are completely unknown to the present men of science.

The Mental Body is enveloped by a silken membrane, which protects it and keeps it in line with the cerebrospinal nervous system. This covering is the Silver Shield of the Mental Body. This shield is completely covered by certain "truncated cones." These are called "modules," which are the senses of the Mental Body.

One among these sensorial centers of the Mental Body permits this body to manipulate the individual and universal seminal currents. There also exists in our Mental Body certain senses which allow us to receive wisdom from distinct stars. The lower counterpart of our Shield forms the convolutions of the brain.

The Mental Body has an atomic nucleus which serves as its base. This nucleus is the Master Atom of the mind. This Master Atom contains the whole wisdom of Nature. Whosoever learns how to be in communication with this atom through meditation will be taught and instructed in the cosmic wisdom, since this atom is a sage.

This Master Atom resides in our seminal system. By practicing Sexual Magic, this atom rises towards our head and then illuminates us in the world of the mind.

The Silver Shield shines like gold when we practice Sexual Magic because millions of transformation atoms of high voltage cover it and totally transform it. Hence, the awakening of the consciousness and the aristocracy of intelligence truly arrive. Then indeed we can talk of having mental erudition and transformational ethics.

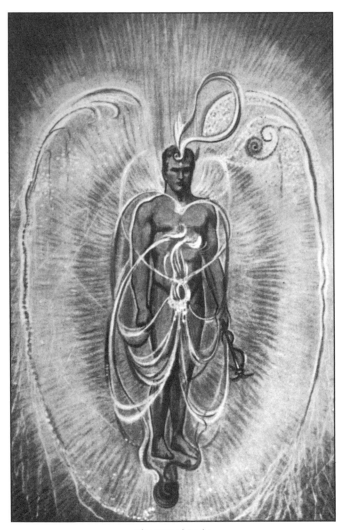

The Mental Body

AS ILLUSTRATED IN "THE DAYSPRING OF YOUTH" BY M.

How can we talk of human sublimation, current achievement and of immediate results without possessing solid mental erudition?

Are perhaps the intimate existent relationships between sexuality and the mind known?

The Psychoanalysis of Sigmund Freud should be studied in order to know the first notions of sexuality in relation with the mind.

Some believe that by playing sports, riding horses or by selecting other sensations, they will get that which pompously is called "the newest conceptions," "mental erudition," "aristocracy of intelligence," and spiritual rebirth.

How can an individual degenerated by the morbidity of carnal passion talk of having a methodical life and complete attention?

How can an individual whose Mental Body still has not been transformed by the Transformation Atoms talk about associations of ideas and of longings?

How can someone who has yet to have the Master Atom on his throne talk of having mental expansion?

How can the oversexed person talk of having a creative mind?

Do they not know that the thoughts which are not penetrated by the Determinative Energy of Nature (sexual energy) become disintegrated?

Do they ignore that the Determinative Energy is the sexual force?

How can an individual whose pineal gland is atrophied because of fornication talk of having courage, willpower, and triumph?

Is it perhaps that the intimate existent relationship between the pineal gland and the sexual glands is unknown, and also because the pineal gland is the messenger of the center of thought?

How can an individual whose brain is weakened, because of the vice of coitus, talk of mental concentration?

How can an individual who has not re-encountered himself and who has become far away from his Innermost due to black magic, talk about personal satisfaction and of being sufficient in oneself?

How can a weak soul be sufficient in itself?

Do they not realize that the souls who are far away from the Innermost are weak souls?

The mind is divided into **concrete mind** and **abstract mind**.

The critique of practical reasoning is one thing and the critique of pure reasoning is another.

The contextual concepts which belong to the critic of practical reasoning are based upon experiences of external sensorial perceptions. Yet, the contextual concepts which belong to the critic of pure reasoning are nourished with prompt ideas and intuition.

The philosophy of Mr. Emmanuel Kant, the great philosopher from Koenissberg, is totally ignored.

Therefore, the systems of "control" and of selection of sensations yearn only for enslaving the disciples of the critic of practical reasoning and the disciples of the inferior mind and concrete mind. Those systems are nothing but pure and legitimate black magic. To convert the disciple into a slave of the exterior sensations and into a black magician is the outcome of such systems.

The **Brahma-Vidya** is the mind of the Innermost.

The mind of the Innermost becomes the fruit or extract of all of the experiences acquired with the Mental Body.

The Brahma-Vidya becomes the aureole body of victory, mentioned in the book *The Dayspring of Youth*.

The mind as a mind is one thing and the mind as an instrument is another. The great cosmic illuminations are the outcome of the momentous unions of Brahma-vidya with the Mental Body. Thus the soul, united with its Innermost, is submerged within the great soul of the world, within Emerson's "super-soul" and perceives all of the macro-cosmic marvels. Yet, in order to achieve these marvels, the opening of the eye of Dangma is necessary. This eye is **intuition**.

The one who is already intuitive is so because he has a specially constructed Mental Body. The nucleus from such a mind is a circle of a resplendent violet color. Within the book *Azug*, the mind which is thus organized is called "Damiorfla."

A Damiorfla person does not bend himself before the potencies of evil, neither is he a slave of maya (illusion).

Whosoever wants to study the book of oriental wisdom entitled *Azug* has first of all to submit himself to great and terrible Initiatic ordeals. I received this book from the hands of the authentic Master of wisdom Kout Humi (K. H.).

So, the system of selecting sensations and piercing the mind with "controls" and more mind controls everyday, only achieves to enslave the disciple to his animal mind and to his no less fatalistic intellect. All of this is nothing but black magic. The only thing which is achieved with these tenebrous teachings is the total separation of the Monad and the personality. Hence, the person ends up despising his Monad and rendering cult to his Guardian of the Threshold, to his internal beast.

Reasoning is one thing and intuition is another. Reasoning only nourishes itself with external sensorial perceptions (by means of the senses it perceives or receives impressions and then produces sensations). Thus, reasoning ends up being negative and limited.

The reasoning person believes that he can attain the truth through the struggle of antithesis, but this struggle only divides the mind and incapacitates its ability to comprehend the truth.

The intuitive person knows how to listen only to the voice of the silence. Thus, within his serene mind, the eternal truths of life are reflected with splendid beauty.

The reasoning person converts his mind into a battlefield filled with prejudices, fears, anxieties, fanaticism, and theories, and his conclusions are always favorable to him. Yet, such a turbulent lake can never reflect the sun of truth.

The mind of the intuitive one serenely and silently flows very far away from the black struggle of antithesis and from the storm of exclusivity.

The mind of the reasoner is like a ship that only knows how to change harbors. From these harbors, which are called schools, theories, religions, political parties, etc., he acts and reacts with already established precepts. A mind like this is a slave of the stagnant energies of life. Therefore, it ends up with complications and pain.

The children of intuition, as rebellious, high flying eagles, soar towards the sun of the great ineffable truths, free from fear, free from the longing of accumulation, free from sects, religions, schools, social prejudices, fanaticism of flags, anxieties, theories, intellectualism, hatred, selfishness, etc.

The mind of the intuitive one serenely and silently flows as a delectable, crystalline fountain of resplendent beauty within the august thunder of thought.

The Mental Body of the intuitive one is a marvelous vehicle of the Innermost. The mind of such an intuitive one only acts under the direction of the Innermost. Hence, from this action emerges right exertion, right thinking, and right feeling.

The human being who only moves himself under the direction of his Innermost in the world is a happy human being because he is far away from many types of complications and conflicts.

In order to reach the ineffable summits of intuition, there is the necessity of integrally living in accordance with the wise teachings brought unto the earth by the Divine Rabbi of Galilee. Therefore, the teachings of Christ are the teachings which lead us towards the ineffable summits of intuition.

What is interesting is to exactly move ourselves in this physical world in accordance with the wise teachings of the Master. What is important is to make the teachings of Christ become flesh and blood within ourselves.

Christ did not come in order to found religions. Christ came so that we could unite ourselves with the Innermost (our eternal Father).

The entire teaching of Christ has the great musical rhythm from the plane of the waves of life, which is the Buddhic or intuitive world.

The mantra **Aum Masi Padme Yum** develops intuition when it is daily vocalized for ten minutes. This mantra is vocalized as follows: *Ooooommmm mmmmaaaa sssssssiiiiiiii paddddddmeeeee yommmmmm.* This is the mantra of intuition.

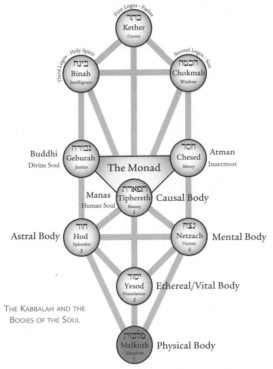

The Kabbalah and the
Bodies of the Soul

The practices of the teaching of Christ awaken the chakra of the heart within us and put into activity the Buddhic or Intuitive body, which leads us towards wisdom and eternal happiness.

Sexual Magic forms part of the teachings which Christ taught to his seventy disciples in secrecy.

While we practice the Christic teachings, the Ethereal (vital) body becomes totally reorganized and its two superior ethers are increased in volume. Then, a certain center which is formed within the head descends into the heart and organizes a center for the intuition.

A protector net is formed around the Ethereal body when we do not waste our Christic force. This is how this body remains protected from the exterior currents. The physical body becomes more fine and also more strong, and even the face is transformed and gains beauty.

The teachings of the Solar Logos operate upon all of our internal bodies, thus converting them into fine instruments of the Innermost. What is important is to live these teachings in our practical life.

Sadly, many people confuse the cosmic mind with the cosmic consciousness. The waves of the mind are one thing and the waves of the consciousness are another.

The mind is nourished by the consciousness.

The cosmic consciousness reunites the affine waves of the mind.

The trident symbolizes the triple set of forces of the Transformation Atoms of the mind.

The Mental Body is not the "I." The Mental Body is only an instrument of the "I." Thus, to pretend to be enslaved by this material instrument is the breaking point of stubbornness.

The mind of the intuitive one is an ineffable chalice filled with beauty.

The mind of the intuitive one is the chalice of the Holy Grail saturated with the blood of the Martyr of Golgotha.

The mind of the intuitive one is the sacred cup of Pleroma, the sacred cup of Samadhi, the liquor of the Gods. It is the Soma, drunk by the Lords of the Mind. It is the liquor of love, the Buddhic liquor, which is the wine of light already transmuted within the igneous vessel of the beautiful Helen. It is the cup of the immortal Gods!

Helen

Hail! Hail Gods immortal,
A toast for Ye, in this delectable chalice
and a toast for the virgin of the seven portals.

A toast for Helen of majestic face
and to her I chant my songs
under the immortal colonnades
of her serene temple.

Helen, fill my cup
with the wine of intuition
Helen, pour within my glass
thy amphora of love...

Helen, console my painful heart.
I want to drink the liquor of wisdom,
even if it would add pain...
I want to inebriate myself with light and poetry
and to awaken in the arms of thy love.

Beautiful Helen, I love thee,
thou art the burin of philosophy,
thou art the fire of the arcane
thou art the amphora of wisdom
and the longed for fiancé of the wise.

The purple and the gold
of ancient Ithaca, I place before thy feet.

Oh Helen!
I place before thy feet the luxury of Atreida.
Oh nubile maiden,
I place before thee the Greek vessels.
Oh serene goddess,
I place before thy feet all the ancient citadels.
Oh beautiful Helen.

Helen, fill my cup
with the wine of intuition,
pour within my glass
thy amphora of love.

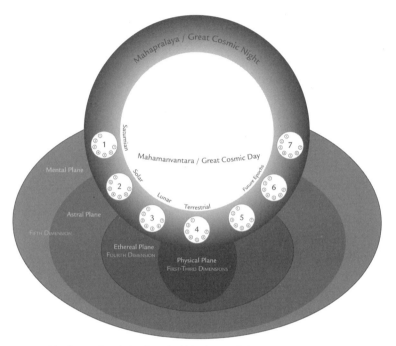

The Lunar Epoch developed within the parallel universe of the fourth
dimension, specifically within the etheric plane.

CHAPTER 9

The Lunar Period

The dawn of the Lunar period began after the passing of the Solar period's cosmic night. Then the solar universe condensed itself into Ethereal matter and life recapitulated all of the states of the past cosmic periods.

The beginning of our Ethereal Earth, which is called the Earth-Moon (the Lunar Period in all of its plenitude), was initiated after those processes of recapitulation.

The human beings of the Lunar epoch were short in stature, and their bodies were of Ethereal matter. They built their houses underground even though they placed roofs on their homes that were similar to those which we place on our present houses. They negotiated, worked, and enjoyed themselves the same way as we do. Their urban populations were small and were connected as our own towns are by avenues and roads.

They also had automobiles similar to our cars. Their mountains were transparent like crystal and were of a very beautiful dark blue, which is like the blue color seen when looking at the mountains from a far off distance (which is the ether). The whole of our ancient Earth was of that beautiful color.

Volcanoes were in incessant eruption, and there was more water than in our present epoch. Immense lakes and vast seas existed everywhere...

In this Lunar period, we see Beelzebub living in an enormous house which was constructed beneath the ground. Here, within a large room, he instructed his disciples, wearing a tunic of black and red stripes, a turban and a cape of the same color. He was a black magician who had a tall and robust body. All of his black chelas (disciples) profoundly venerated him.

Beelzebub had two books: One book which he read to his disciples in order to instruct them, and the other that only he studied in secret. There were many proselytes among the human beings of the Lunar period which he conquered for black magic.

The flora and fauna of that time were very different from our own. Here we clairvoyantly see plant-minerals, that is to say, semi-plants, semi-minerals, semi-animal plants, etc. In other words, the three kingdoms of Nature were not completely defined as in the present time, since in that epoch one kingdom was integrated with the other.

Among the trees there was the marked tendency for the branches and leaves to make a concave shape, which caused them to resemble gigantic umbrellas. Through all existent things, this marked tendency of inclining downwards was Nature's living scripture foreseen everywhere. Its process downwards was towards the condensation of our present physical Earth. Nature is a living scripture everywhere; therefore, its designs are written based on this living scripture.

On the other hand, we see in our present epoch, in this XX century, a marked tendency of the human being to build very high buildings and airplanes, each time more and more rapidly, etc.

The branches of our contemporary trees do not want to incline downwards, instead they want to elevate themselves upwards to the sun. This is because our earth has already reached its maximum material condensation, and now it yearns to elevate itself anew, to "Etherealize" itself again... Really, the ether is inundating the air and Etherealizing the Earth each time, more and more. Thus, at the end of the great Aryan Root Race, the ether will be totally visible in the air. Then, all the creatures who live in the ether will share all of their activities with the human being.

During the Lunar period, the physical bodies of our present humanity reached a high degree in their perfection. We acquired the Astral Body during that period.

We, the human beings of present times, were the animals of the Lunar period. The angels and demons of ancient periods floated in the Ethereal atmosphere of our Earth-Moon. They were visible and tangible to the whole of that humanity.

Those human beings perceived the Archangels (Archengeloi) or Creatures of Fire behind the erupted fire of volcanoes and the Lords of Formation behind all of the existent forms.

The Children of Life regulated the vital functions of every existent thing, and the elemental creatures of the five elements of Nature coexisted with the human beings.

The Lords of Wisdom were the ones who endowed us with the Astral Body. The Lords of the Personality were the ones who endowed us with personality, which at this present time is despised by the Theosophists.

The Innermosts (Monad-Spirits) of this present humanity acquired the body of the Human Spirit, called the Body of Willpower, which Krishnamurti despised so much.

Willpower is the power with which we can dominate our passions in order to convert ourselves into Gods.

When the law of the Gnostic Alchemist is accomplished (the introduction of the virile member into the feminine vagina and its withdrawal without spilling the semen), then the fire of passion is transmuted into Astral Light. This is how the Astral Body is strengthened and is filled with resplendent light.

F.   SOLVTIO PERFECTA   III.

The conjunction of the male and female energies is the "perfect solution."
FROM DONUM DEI, 17TH CENTURY

Therefore, all of the resplendent fruits of this marvelous Astral organism are plunged within the Body of Willpower, which beautifies it.

The fire of chastity is the fire of the Holy Spirit, and the body of the Holy Spirit is the Body of Willpower, also called Abstract Mind and Causal Body.

Really, the body of the Abstract Mind is converted into the Fire of Pentecost when inundated with fire by means of Sexual Magic. It utters ineffable things in all the languages of the world within the speechless

human who is inebriated with the Holy Spirit. It is what the Holy Gnostic Bible textually states:

> *And when the day of Pentecost was fully come, they were all with one accord in one place.*
>
> *And suddenly there came a sound from heaven as of a rushing mighty wind, and it filled all the house where they were sitting.*
>
> *And there appeared unto them cloven tongues like as of fire, and it sat upon each of them.*
>
> *And they were all filled with the Holy Ghost, and began to speak with other tongues, as the Spirit gave them utterance.*
>
> THE ACTS OF THE APOSTLES, 2: 1-6

Jehovah, the Holy Spirit, guards the body of the Holy Spirit in ourselves. Jehovah was the highest Initiate from the Lunar epoch.

Humanity was divided into angels and lucifers when that great period ended, since many are called, but few are chosen.

Max Heindel and Rudolf Steiner affirm in their books that all of humanity will be saved. This is due to the ignorance of these authors. Verses 23, 24, 25, 26, 27 and 28 of the 13th chapter of Luke textually say:

> *Then said one unto him, Lord, are there few that be saved? And he said unto them,*

> *Strive to enter in at the strait gate: for many, I say unto you, will seek to enter in, and shall not be able.*

> *When once the master of the house is risen up, and hath shut to the door, and ye begin to stand without, and to knock at the door, saying Lord, Lord open unto us: and he shall answer and say unto you, I know you not whence ye are:*

> *Then ye shall begin to say, we have eaten and drunk in thy presence, and thou hast taught in our streets.*

> *But he shall say, I tell you, I know you not whence ye are; depart from me, all ye workers of iniquity.*

> *There shall be weeping and gnashing of teeth, when ye shall see Abraham, and Isaac, and Jacob, and all of the Prophets, in the kingdom of God, and you yourselves thrust out.*

When the cosmic night of the Lunar period arrived, Jehovah and his angels, Lucifer and his demons, withdrew themselves from the cosmic scenario. Thus, the whole of Nature entered into a profound repose.

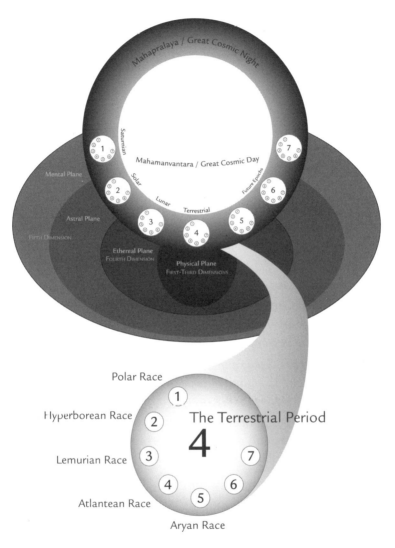

The Terrestrial Epoch is the current period which is developing within the universe of the third dimension, specifically in the physical plane.

CHAPTER 10
The Terrestrial Period

When the cosmic night of the Lunar period had passed, the universe condensed into a nebula, as referred to by Laplace. It was the beginning of this physical-chemical epoch in which we presently live.

Nature recapitulated all of the former cosmic periods, which are allegorically described in Genesis:

> In the beginning God created the heaven and the earth. And the earth was without form, and void; and darkness was upon the face of the deep. And the Spirit of God moved upon the face of the waters. GENESIS 1:1-2

These were the times of Laplace's nebula during which the earth recapitulated the Saturnian epoch.

> And God said let there be light: and there was light. And God saw the light, that it was good: and God divided the light from the darkness. GENESIS 1:3-4

Then, the molecules of the dark heat nebula entered into friction under the powerful impulse of the lost word of the Creator, and this nebula ignited and became luminous.

This was the Hyperborean epoch during which the solar atoms from the Solar epoch entered into activity. Our Earth was an igneous globe filled with the wisdom of the fire, and with the light that the same fire produces. Thus, the Archangels (who were the human beings of the Solar epoch) were the beings who lived within this fiery globe. They expressed themselves with all of the plenitude of their wisdom.

> And God said, let there be a firmament in the midst of the waters, and let it divide the waters from the waters. And God made the firmament, and divided the waters which were under the firmament from the waters which were above the firmament: and it was so. And God called the firmament Heaven. And the evening and the morning were the second day. GENESIS 1:5-8

Here the Bible keeps referring to the recapitulation of the Solar period. Moisture was generated by the contact of this igneous globe with the surrounding interplanetary regions, which are cold. Enormous clouds were condensed, gravitating back to the source of heat in the form of rain; enormous seas and wells were formed, incessantly boiling upon the fiery globe. Thus, the clouds separated the waters of heaven from the waters of the fiery globe:

> And God said, let the waters under the heaven be gathered together unto one place, and let the dry land appear: and it was so. And God called the dry land Earth; and the gathering together of the waters called He seas; and God saw that it was good.
> GENESIS: 1: 9-10

The incessant boiling of the water wells surrounding the fiery core finally caused encrustation and dry land appeared upon the surface of the fiery globe. Thus, the word of the Creator was accomplished when He said, *"and let the dry land appear... And God called the dry land Earth."* This is how the first terrestrial crust called Lemuria was formed.

During this Lemurian epoch, the Earth recapitulated the Lunar period because the following law in life exists: before initiating its new manifestations, Nature has to recapitulate all of its former manifestations.

Therefore, whosoever wants to objectively know all of the evolving processes of humanity has to observe the human fetus from its very conception. Within the maternal womb, the human fetus recapitulates the whole metamorphosis of the human body from its very ancient origins.

The human body is nothing else but the scale of our igneous serpent. Thus, the solar universe is only the scale of the serpent of the Solar Logos of this Solar System.

When the serpent abandons the scale, the scale is disintegrated (this igneous serpent is the Kundalini, referred to in the chapter entitled the *Staff of the Patriarchs*).

The Mountain of Juratena

There exists in Colombia a very high mountain named "The Juratena." This mountain is situated in the Vasquez territory, state of Bocaya. It is at the shore of the broad and profound waters of a river named Minero.

The peasants say that the mountain is "enchanted." They tell the most ancient traditions about it. They say that when it is going to rain they feel the noise of enormous rocky boulders which roll towards the abyss, and when they want rain, it is enough for them to light the mountain with fire in order to have rain in abundance.

These peasants do not care a bit about the commentaries of scientists regarding these matters. As Goethe has stated: "Every theory is grey and only the tree of the golden fruits of life is green."

These peasants narrate that the summit of this mountain is accessible through some high steps of rock which were carved by very ancient hands. One of these peasants was telling the author of this current book how he was stopped by a rain of rocks thrown by invisible hands when drawing near to these millinery high steps. He was close to perishing under the rolling weight of a gigantic boulder which almost squashed him.

Another peasant explored the base of the mountain while following the course of the broad and profound waters of the river. He happened upon enormous boulders of granite which were bathed by the boisterous waters of the river, and then he found a gigantic temple inlayed within the living rock. This peasant tried to enter into the temple through the central door (since this gigantic temple had three doors), but he found himself surrounded by many serpent skins. Consequently, he flew away terrified. Later on, he returned to this place in order to see the temple; yet, he did not find anything. That temple had disappeared as if it had been swallowed by those gigantic rocks.

I, Samael Aun Weor, visited that temple in my Astral Body. The Masters who dwell there welcomed me with open arms. They lead me towards the interior of this monastery, which was illuminated by a seven armed candelabra of massive gold, similar to the seven armed candelabra of gold from the temple of Solomon. I then received from them secret teachings.

Theosophists believe that the Masters are only in Tibet, and some of them would like to travel there in order to follow the "chela-hood" (fellowship). Yet, the monasteries of the White Lodge are sprouting up all over the world.

In the east, the Mahatmas are called "Nagas," that is to say, "serpents." This is why all of the guardians from the sacred crypts of the temples of mysteries have the figures of gigantic serpents who only allow Initiates to enter.

The poison of a snake kills; yet, we can arrive at the High Initiation with this poison, which is a "precious arcanum." Listen to me, Initiate Reader, "the hiss of the snake is the base of life." This statement is not for all readers; therefore, *"He that hath an ear, let him hear."*

The inhabitants of "tierra llana," state of Zulia, Venezuela, make the serpents flee when they pronounce the following mantras:

Ooooooooooooo Sssssssssssssssss Iiiiiiiiiiiiiiiiiiiii

Ooooooooo Ssssssssssss Ooooooooo Aaaaaaaaaaa

Aaaaaaaaaaaaaaaa Ssssssssssssssss Iiiiiiiiiiiiiiiiiiiii

The vowels of these mantras are **I.A.O.** which are combined with the tremendous letter **S**. *"Here is wisdom; let him that hath understanding, understand."*

Even though grammarians do not say so, the letter **S** is also a vowel.

We have to pronounce the three vowels **I.A.O.** together with the priestess-wife, while connected during Sexual Magic, because **I.A.O.** is the name of our serpent...

To clarify this chapter, we will say this: the Polar epoch corresponds to the Mercurial Intelligence of the serpent of the Logos (the heat).

The Hyperborean epoch corresponds to the serpent's solar atoms (the fire).

The Lemurian epoch corresponds to the lunar atoms of the serpent of the Logos (the humidity).

Our Kundalini is also formed from solar and lunar atoms and from a synthesis of omniscient atoms. Hence, the wisdom of seven eternities is integrated within the serpent.

The woman is the vestal of the temple; thus, the fire of the temple is lit by the vestal. In ancient times, the fire was guarded and lit by the vestals. This symbolizes that only the woman has the unique capability of lighting her husband's fire of Kundalini, which is the fire from our body or our temple. The temple of the very high, living God is our body and the fire of this temple is the Kundalini, which our vestal-spouse lights by means of the same sexual contact, or Sexual Magic, as taught in the book *The Perfect Matrimony or the Door to Enter into Initiation,* and as well within this current book.

In this present time, the Roman Catholic Church has totally lost this tradition. That is why we see that in this Roman Church the fire of the temple is lit by acolyte boys, an action that is not only an absurdity, but moreover, a very grave sacrilege and an insult to life itself.

Continuing on, we say that the former cosmic periods actually exist within our seminal atoms and it is merely enough to learn the technique of interior meditation to enter into their dominions.

The door to enter into those powerful atomic civilizations is in our sexual organs.

The pralayas and manvantaras are happening within an always eternal instant. Past and future are joined within an eternal now.

Time does not exist! It is the mind of the human being that is in charge of dividing the eternal now into past and future!

The powerful Saturnian, Solar, and Lunar civilizations still exist in the depths of our seminal system. We can enter into their dominions by means of interior meditation. The transition of the consciousness from one state into another is what we erroneously call "time," but these states of consciousness are in a successive enchainment within an eternal now.

Therefore, the human being must learn to always live in the present, liberating himself from all types of pompous theosophy, religious sectarianism, country and flag fanaticism, religions, intellectualism, yearning for accumulation and general attachments. All of these hedonistic parrot cages are nothing but dens of business and tyranny. We gain nothing from their gibberish, because they serve only to fill us with prejudices and absurd fanaticism!

The entire wisdom of all ages is within ourselves. Past and future are joined within an eternal now!

All of the cosmic wisdom is within ourselves. The solar atoms initiate us into the wisdom of the fire. The lunar atoms initiate us into the very ancient Neptunian-Amentine wisdom. When these solar and lunar atoms make contact, the sacred fire awakens and we convert ourselves into Gods.

During nights of the full moon, the lunar atoms make contact with the Silver Shield of our Mental Body. At that time we are able to receive the teachings of the lunar wisdom by means of meditation. Seven lunar Ethereal currents exist. The civilization of our ancient Earth-Moon intensely lives within them.

The solar and lunar civilizations live within our interior worlds and we can visit those civilizations by means of profound interior meditation.

The solar and lunar civilizations, which intensely palpitate within our own internal worlds, initiate us into their profound truths. They take us to the great illumination by means of the awakening of the sacred fire of Kundalini through Sexual Magic.

Our seven chakras are seven internal churches and each one of these seven churches contains the wisdom of a cosmic period. When we have opened the seven seals from the seven churches of the human book with the sword of the Kundalini, then the seven churches deliver to us the whole cosmic wisdom of the seven cosmic periods of the Mahamanvantara. This is how we become omniscient...

The Book of the Apocalypse (Revelation) says the following:

> And when he had opened the seventh seal, there was silence in heaven about the space of half an hour.
>
> And I saw the seven angels which stood before God; and to them were given seven trumpets.
>
> And another angel came and stood at the altar, having a golden censer and there was given unto him much incense that he should offer it with the prayers of all saints upon the golden altar which was before the throne.
>
> And the smoke of the incense which came with the prayers of the saints, ascended up before God out of the angel's hand.
>
> REVELATION 8:1-4

THE SEVEN ANGELS

Here, the Apocalypse refers to the book sealed with seven seals, the book that is within our organism with its seven churches. It clearly tells us that only the Lamb can open its seven seals with the sword of the Kundalini.

The Lamb is our interior Angel, that is to say, our Innermost. When the seventh seal is opened (the seal that is related with the church of Laodicea, situated on the head) then the Lamb teaches that the seven Angels of the seven trumpets are the same seven Angels of the seven churches.

The Angel with the golden censer is our Innermost, who triumphantly enters into the White Hierarchy along with his Diamond Soul. He becomes another Perfect One among the community of the Elected Ones...

> *And the angel took the censer, and filled it with the fire of the altar, and cast it into the earth: and there were voices, and thunderings, and lightnings, and an earthquake.* REVELATION 8:5

Here the Apocalypse tells us that when we have opened the seventh seal with the sword of the Kundalini, then the seven churches open their doors for us and teach us the wisdom of the seven great terrestrial periods, which correspond to the seven great cosmic periods.

The eighth chapter of the Apocalypse continues referring to the seven Angels, stating that when they consecutively sound their respective trumpets, the great cosmic events are successively occurring.

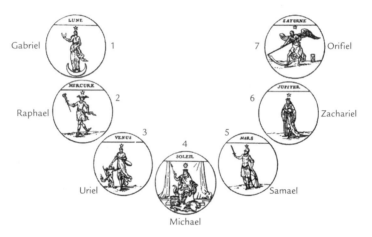

These seven Angels are the Angels of our seven planets who direct the seven chakras of our organism and also the seven terrestrial epochs.

Therefore, the seven terrestrial epochs are directed by seven cosmic hierarchies and the whole wisdom of all of these seven epochs is within our seven chakras... Our terrestrial period has seven epochs.

> *And I saw another mighty angel come down from heaven, clothed with a cloud; and a rainbow was upon his head, and his face was as it were the sun, and his feet as pillars of fire:*
>
> *And he had in his hand a little book open: and he set his right foot upon the sea, and his left foot on the earth.*

And cried with a loud voice, as when a lion roareth: and when he had cried, seven thunders uttered their voices. REVELATION 10:1-3

This Angel is the hierarch of the seventh epoch. The rainbow symbolizes our present terrestrial period, which started with the rainbow (Genesis 9:12-13). This happened in Atlantis, because Lemuria was a recapitulation of the Lunar period.

The little book that the Angel had in his hand is the book of human evolution. It is the book sealed with seven seals; yet, it is the book already without seals. It is the human organism of the one who has already opened the seven seals - it is the body of the Master. It is the cosmic wisdom of the one who has already reached deep realization of the Self.

And cried with a loud voice, as when a lion roareth: and when he had cried, seven thunders uttered their voices. REVELATION 10:3

Here the Apocalypse tells us about the lost word, about the sacred syllable that the seven thunders of the seven chakras uttered with their voices. These voices are the seven notes of the lost word. The sacred syllable opens the seven chakras and so each chakra has its own keynote. *"He that has an ear, let him hear. Here is wisdom. Let him that has understanding understand."*

The lost word shall be found in the seventh epoch.

And when the seven thunders had uttered their voices, I was about to write: and I heard a voice from heaven saying unto me, "Seal up those things which the seven thunders uttered, and write them not." REVELATION 10:4

Each note of the lost word encloses tremendous unutterable secrets. Each note of the lost word is the keynote of a terrestrial epoch. Thus, the keynote of the Egyptian civilization is one note, and another is the keynote of the Hindustani civilization, and so forth, successively.

In the days of the seventh epoch, the lost word shall fulfill completely the mystery of the kingdom of God. The Swedish mystic-philosopher Swedenborg said the following when referring to the lost word: "Search for it in China, and maybe you will find it in the great Tartar."

The black magicians of Sodom use the mantra "Mathra" (they pronounce it Mazra) for their demonic goals. They assert to their disciples that "Mathra" is the lost word; yet, in reality, this word is the name of a temple of black magic of ancient Atlantis and is at the same time a mantra for black magic. Thus, "Mathra" is not the lost word.

In India, the Arahats were persecuted because they possessed the sacred syllable. In China, the disciples of Tathagata possess the lost word.

In Tibet, the lost word is very well protected, for here is where the Maha-Choan abides.

The lost word shall be found in the seventh epoch.

> But in the days of the voice of the seventh angel, when he shall begin to sound, the mystery of God should be finished, as he had declared to his servants the prophets.
>
> And sware by him that liveth for ever and ever, who created heaven, and the things that therein are, and the earth, and the things that therein are, and the sea, and the things that are therein, that there should be time no longer. REVELATION 10:6, 7

The Initiate who is already united with his Innermost is liberated from the illusion of time, because past and future are joined within an eternal now.

Each one of the seven terrestrial epochs finishes with a great cataclysm, which is symbolically described in the Apocalypse in the following way:

> And the first angel sounded, and there followed hail and fire mingled with blood, and they were cast upon earth: and the third part of the trees was burnt up, and all green grass was burnt up. REVELATION 8:7

This was the first cataclysm of the first epoch.

> And the second angel sounded, and as it were a great mountain burning with fire was cast into the sea: and the third part of the sea became blood;
>
> And the third part of the creatures which were in the sea, and had life, died, and the third part of the ships were destroyed. REVELATION 8:8-9

This was the end of the second epoch.

And the third angel sounded, and there fell a great star from heaven, burning as it were a lamp, and it fell upon the third part of the rivers, and upon the fountains of waters;

And the name of the star is called Wormwood and the third part of the waters became wormwood; and many men died of the waters, because they were made bitter. REVELATION 8:10-11

This was the end of the third epoch.

And the fourth angel sounded, and the third part of the sun was smitten, and the third part of the moon, and the third part of the stars; so as the third part of them was darkened, and the day shone not for a third part of it, and the night likewise. REVELATION 8:12

This was the end of the fourth epoch.

And the fifth angel sounded, and I saw a star fall from heaven unto the earth: and to him was given the key of the bottomless pit.

And he opened the bottomless pit; and there arose a smoke out of the pit, as the smoke of a great furnace; and the sun and the air were darkened by reason of the smoke of the pit. REVELATION 9:1-2

The abyss is the Avitchi, which is a submerged plane of consciousness, where only the weeping and gnashing of teeth are heard. Here enter the souls who have horns on their foreheads. The horns on the forehead are the mark of the beast. In this present time, the abyss is open and millions of demonic souls are entering into the abyss.

And they had a king over them, which is the angel of the bottomless pit, whose name in the Hebrew tongue is Abbadon, but in the Greek tongue hath his name Apollyon. REVELATION 9:11

We are in the epoch of wars because they are necessary, since war produces millions of dead. Thus, the souls who have horns on their forehead enter into the abyss. (Any clairvoyant can see the demonic souls).

And the sixth angel sounded, and I heard a voice from the four horns of the golden altar which is before God.

Saying to the sixth angel which had the trumpet, Loose the four angels which are bound in the great river Euphrates.

The suffering of the abyss.
ENGRAVING BY GUSTAVE DORÉ.

*And the four angels were loosed, which were prepared for an hour,
and a day, and a month, and a year, for to slay the third part of
men.* REVELATION 9:13-15

This will be the sixth epoch. In that epoch the human demons
will be taken into the abyss again, after a very good opportunity for
progress has been given to them.

*And the seventh angel sounded; and there were great voices
in heaven, saying, The kingdoms of this world are become the
kingdoms of our Lord, and of his Christ; and he shall reign for
ever and ever.* REVELATION 11:15

In those future times, the Earth will be more Ethereal and only
the human beings who have reached the angelic state will live in it,
because the millions of demonic souls will definitively go into the
abyss where they will be disintegrated throughout the ages. This
is the Second Death!

CHAPTER 11

Lemuria

*And Jehovah Elohim planted a garden eastward in Eden; and
there he put the man whom he had formed.* Genesis 2:8

There has been much discussion regarding the topic of the
terrestrial paradise. Max Heindel sustained that the terrestrial
paradise is the Astral Light; yet, he did not inquire into what the
word "terrestrial" signifies.

Really, this paradise existed and was the continent of Lemuria,
which was situated in the Pacific Ocean. It was the first dry land
that existed in the world. The temperature during that time was
extremely warm.

*But there went up a mist from the earth, and watered the whole
face of the ground.* Genesis 2:6

The very intense heat together with the water mist created a
foggy atmosphere. Consequently, human beings breathed through
gills like fish.

*So, Elohim created man in his own image, in the image of God
created he him; male and female created he them.* Genesis 1:27

The human beings of the Polar epoch, the Hyperborean
epoch, and even in the beginning of the Lemurian epoch were
hermaphrodites. They reproduced themselves as hermaphroditic
microbes reproduce themselves.

In the earliest times of Lemuria, there was almost no
differentiation between the human species and the animal species.
Yet, after 150,000 years of evolution, the Lemurians reached a very
grand degree of civilization, which we, the Aryans, are still very far
from reaching.

It was the Age of Gold; it was the age of the Titans. It was the
delectable time of Arcadia, a time in which "what is mine and what
is yours" did not exist, because everything belonged to everybody.
It was the time in which the rivers poured forth milk and honey.

The imagination of the human being was an ineffable mirror
in which the panorama of the starry heavens of Urania was
solemnly reflected. The human being knew that his life was the

life of the gods. The one who knew how to play the lyre shook the divine fields with his delectable melodies. The artist who handled the brush inspired himself with the eternal wisdom. He gave to his delicate sculptures the tremendous majesty of God.

Oh, the epoch of the Titans! It was an epoch in which the rivers poured forth milk and honey.

The Lemurians were of a high stature and they had a broad forehead. They wore symbolic tunics, which were white in the front and black in the back. They had flying ships and boats propelled by atomic energy. The lighting system used in the Lemurian structures was made from nuclear energy. They reached a very high degree of culture.

Such were the times of Arcadia. The human being knew how to listen to the voice of the gods through the seven vowels of Nature.

The seven vowels **I.E.O.U.A.M.S.** resounded in the Lemurian bodies with all of the ineffable music of the accentuated rhythms of the fire.

The Gnostic disciple must vocalize the vowels for one hour daily in the described written order. Each vowel must be prolonged as follows, emptying the lungs with each intonation.

Iiiiiiiiiiiiiiiiii, Eeeeeeeeeee, Oooooooooooo, Uuuuuuuuuu, Aaaaaaaaaa, Mmmmmmm, Sssssssssss.

The letter **I** makes the pituitary and the pineal glands vibrate; thus, the human being becomes clairvoyant.

The letter **E** makes the thyroid gland vibrate; thus the human being becomes clairaudient.

The letter **O** makes the chakra of the heart vibrate; thus the human being becomes intuitive.

The letter **U** awakes the solar plexus (top of the stomach); thus, the human being awakens telepathy.

The letter **A** makes the chakra of the lungs vibrate; thus, the human being acquires the power of remembering his past lives.

The vowels **M** and **S** efficiently help in the development of all of the occult powers.

EDITOR'S NOTE: The vowels are pronounced as in Spanish. I as in "tree," E as in "fell," O as in "low," U as in "you," A as in "all."

The human beings performed the sexual connubii under the commands of the Elohim...

ENGRAVING BY GUSTAVE DORÉ

Therefore, one hour of daily vocalization is worth more than reading a million books of oriental theosophy.

The body of the Lemurians was a miraculous harp where the seven vowels of nature sounded with the tremendous euphoria of the cosmos.

When night arrived, all of the human beings fell asleep as innocent creatures within the cradle of Mother Nature. They were lulled with the very sweet and moving chant of the gods. Thus, when the dawn was rising, the sun brought diaphanous contentment and not tenebrous grief.

Oh the epoch of the Titans! Those were the times in which the rivers poured forth milk and honey.

The matrimonies of Arcadia were Gnostic matrimonies. Then, the human beings performed the sexual connubii under the commands of the Elohim as a sacrifice on the altar of matrimony, in order to provide bodies to the souls who needed to reincarnate. Fornication was completely unknown and there was no pain in giving birth.

Throughout many thousands of years, Lemuria sank within the boisterous waves of the Pacific Ocean; meanwhile, the Atlantean continent was emerging from the bottom of the ocean.

And there was war in heaven...

ENGRAVING BY GUSTAVE DORÉ

CHAPTER 12

The War in Heaven

*And there was war in heaven: Michael and his angels fought
against the dragon; and the dragon fought and his angels.*

*And prevailed not; neither was their place found any more in
heaven.*

*And the great dragon was cast out, that old serpent called the
Devil, and Satan, which deceiveth the whole world: he was cast
out into the earth, and his angels were cast out with him.*

*Therefore rejoice, ye heavens, and ye that dwell in them. Woe to
the inhabiters of the earth and of the sea! For the devil is come
down unto you, having great wrath, because he knoweth that he
hath but a short time.* Revelation 12:7-9, 12

There have been two wars against the black magicians: first,
the war in Arcadia, and second, the one in the year 1950, the date in
which the pit of the abyss was opened. The latter is the war related
with the millennium. The third war will be the one related with
the new Jerusalem.

When the terrestrial period was initiated, the mental plane and
even the most divine planes of consciousness were densely super-
populated by every type of white and black magician who belonged
to the Saturnine, Solar, and Lunar periods.

The millions of black magicians constituted gigantic
populations of evil that were obstructing the action and life of the
White Magicians. Hence, they were already a grave inconvenience
for cosmic evolution within the superior worlds of consciousness.

If life had continued in that way, then the progression of
aspirants toward the superior worlds would have been impossible.

Therefore, the White Fraternity gave the mission of casting
out all of the black magicians from the superior planes of
consciousness to Michael. He received the Sword of Justice and
tremendous powers were granted to him so that he could totally
accomplish his mission.

All of the organizations of the Black Lodge and all of the
temples of that tenebrous fraternity were established in the

superior planes of consciousness. Michael was able to perform this mission due to the fact that he belonged to the Ray of Power.

So, Michael fought in tremendous combats, hand to hand with the terrible hierarchies of the Black Lodge. This is how the great Dragon, the old serpent called the Demon, Satan, or black magic with all of its legions of demons, was cast out of the superior planes of consciousness by Michael.

Luzbel is a great hierarch of the Black Lodge. He wears a red cape and a tunic of the same color. His tail or Kundabuffer is extremely long, and he carries at the end of it a coiled papyrus on which is written the science of evil. The tail of the demons is formed when the current of the Kundalini is directed downwards towards the

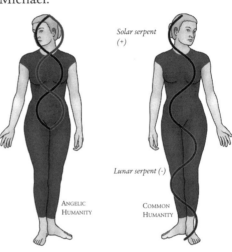

Solar serpent (+)

Lunar serpent (-)

ANGELIC HUMANITY

COMMON HUMANITY

infernos of the human being. Therefore, this tail is nothing but the Kundalini itself that has departed downwards from the coccyx.

The horns of every black magician are certainly the mark of the beast. These horns belong to the Guardian of the Threshold, who becomes the superior "I" of the black magician.

Ariman, a great black hierarch, wears a red turban and he is chief of enormous legions. Lucifer was the greatest black Initiate from the Lunar epoch; his legions are numerous.

All of these millions of demons remained in the environment of our Earth. They dedicated themselves to placing all of the human souls on the way of the black path.

Beelzebub, with his legions, also established himself in our environment. He became very well known by all of the present human beings throughout time. In the Bible, Beelzebub is called the God of Ekron, because a temple was built for him in Ekron, and he was worshipped there as a god. (2 Kings 1:2)

So, Beelzebub established his cavern and dedicated himself fully, as in the ancient periods, to mislay the souls.

The Bible refers to Beelzebub in Matthew, chapter twelve, verses 24-27, as follows:

> But when the Pharisees heard it, they said, This fellow doth not cast out devils, but by Beelzebub the prince of the devils.
>
> And Jesus knew their thoughts, and said unto them, Every kingdom divided against itself is brought to desolation; and every city or house divided against itself shall not stand:
>
> And if Satan cast out Satan, he is divided against himself; how shall then his kingdom stand?
>
> And if I by Beelzebub cast out devils, by whom do your children cast them out? Therefore they shall be your judges.

All of the black magicians established their temples, lodges, halls, cults etc., on our Earth, and they dedicated themselves to developing their plans in accordance with the supreme commands of Javhe.

Therefore, they are responsible for the failure of our present human evolution, since it is a terrible reality that this present human evolution has failed.

Michael triumphed in the heavens, but our Earth was filled with profound darkness.

Woe to the inhabitants of the earth!

During great earthquakes, Atlantis sank with all of its black magicians
to the bottom of the Atlantic Ocean.

ENGRAVING BY GUSTAVE DORÉ

CHAPTER 13
Atlantis

The human beings of Atlantis reached a very high degree in their civilization, similar to that of the Lemurians. During that time, the Earth was enveloped by a thick mist, and the human beings breathed through gills. The Lemurian flying ships and boats propelled with atomic energy were also known in Atlantis.

In the beginning of this civilization, sexual relations were only performed with the objective of engendering bodies for reincarnating souls. The proper day and hour was chosen by the angels, and for this reason childbearing was painless. Human beings were living in a paradisiacal state; yet, Lucifer and the lucifers, the black magicians from the Lunar period, tempted the human being, and they misled him towards the black path.

The serpent is the sexual force, and not simply material attraction, as supposed by the Rosicrucians in their monographs of the ninth degree.

The sexual force has two poles: positive and negative. The positive is the serpent of bronze which healed the Israelites in the wilderness. The negative is the tempting serpent of Eden.

The work of the lucifers was a work of black magic. They awoke the passionate fire of humanity with the single purpose of creating proselytes for the Black Lodge, since every demon is a fornicator.

The cephalic-rachis liquid and the semen are the poles of the sexual energy. The angel has the two poles upwards, towards his head. The common and current human beings and the demons have one pole upward and the other downward. They form the brain with one pole, and they fornicate with the other pole.

The Kundalini of the angel goes upwards; yet, the demon's Kundabuffer goes downwards.

Jehovah prohibited fornication to man; yet, Lucifer seduced him towards it.

And Jehovah Elohim commanded the man saying, Of every tree of the garden thou mayest freely eat:

But of the tree of the knowledge of good and evil, thou shall not eat of it: for in the day that thou eatest thereof thou shalt surely die.
GENESIS 2:16-17

And the serpent said unto the woman, Ye shall not surely die.

For God doth know that in the day ye eat thereof, then your eyes shall be opened, and ye shall be as gods, knowing good and evil.
GENESIS 3:4-5

The commandment given by Jehovah is White Magic. The commandment given by Lucifer is black magic.

When the human being delivered himself to the pleasures of coitus, he lost his occult powers. Thus, the words of Jehovah were accomplished when he said:

In the sweat of thy face shall thou eat bread, till thou return unto the ground; for out of it wast thou taken; for dust thou art, and unto dust shalt thou return.   GENESIS 3:19

Unto the woman he said, I will greatly multiply thy sorrow and thy conception; in sorrow thou shall bring forth children; and thy desire shall be to thy husband, and he shall rule over thee.
GENESIS 3:16

The violation of any law always brings pain. Childbearing was painless for the women in Lemuria, because the child was engendered in the very hour, minute, and second which the cosmic laws favored for reproduction. Thus, the violation of this law brought pain in childbirth.

Nonetheless, in this day and age there is still a remedy for those who resolve to follow the Gnostic matrimony.

The Gnostic matrimony returns the human being to paradise. In the Gnostic Church, the Gnostic matrimonies receive the exact day, hour, and minute in which they have to engender their children. Thus, there is no pain in childbirth. What is important is to know how to travel in the Astral Body in order to visit the Gnostic Temple. I will give these clues later on.

The Lemurians did not know death. They knew the exact date and hour of their disincarnation, and so they dug their own tombs. They abandoned their own body by will and with a smile on their lips.

Childbearing was painless for the women in Lemuria, because the child
was engendered in the very hour, minute and second which the cosmic
laws favored for reproduction.

They also never disappeared from the sight of their relatives,
because they were clairvoyant. They kept coexisting with the dead
because death was simply a passing into a different state. But
when the human being lost his powers because of coitus, then he
knew death.

The Gnostic places all of his longings in the
hands of his Innermost.

ENGRAVING BY GUSTAVE DORÉ

CHAPTER 14

Black Magic of the Atlanteans

The black magicians of the school of Sodom say that black magic does not exist, that it is only a superstition. They say that the evil and hateful thoughts which are emitted by evil minds are disintegrated since "the cosmos" is pure goodness. Therefore, it cannot serve as an instrument for the forces of evil.

The goal of the above noted statement of the black magicians from the school of Sodom is to justify their tenebrous teachings in order to give them the false appearance of being pure White Magic.

The cosmos is the whole Infinite, and in the cosmos there are many things. As above, so below.

If a thought, which is emitted by an evil one, is disintegrated at once, why then is not a bullet disintegrated in the atmosphere? Why does the cosmos serve as an instrument for a bullet, which is going to kill a human being who might be an elder or a child?

If that concept of the black magicians from the school of Sodom is true, then the bullet would disintegrate itself at once.

Possibly they would argue by saying to me that the bullet is a material body and a thought is not. Yet, this is also not a good explanation because thought is also matter. Nothing can exist, not even God, without the help of matter.

Moreover, every atom is septuple in its constitution. The bullet used as an example is a compound of physical, Ethereal, Astral, Mental, Causal, Conscientious, and Divine atoms. In other words, the bullet is a nucleus of atomic consciousness, which is charged with the waves of hatred from the one who shot it.

Why then is the bullet not disintegrated? Why does the cosmos serve as an instrument for the bullet?

Why does the cosmos serve as an instrument for the destructive waves of the atomic bomb? Is it conceivable that mental waves are inferior to the radioactive waves of the atoms of uranium?

Hence, that concept of the black magicians from the school of Sodom serves them in order to conceal their crimes and cheat naive people. The only thing they want is to justify themselves as White Magicians.

Do not covet powers, beloved reader. Powers are born as fruits of our Innermost when our soul has been purified. The mental force that we stubbornly use in order to move a piece of paper would be better used in order to dominate our carnal passion, in order to end hatred, in order to dominate our language, in order to defeat selfishness, envy, etc.

Let us purify ourselves, since powers will be granted to us through successive purifications. Powers are flowers of the soul and fruits of the Innermost. The powers of a Mahatma are the fruits of millinery purifications.

The Gnostic disciple receives distinct powers from the White Lodge through the Initiatic ordeals. These powers are acquired by the soul and the Innermost "seizes" them because the Innermost is the real human within us.

For instance, when the Gnostic wishes a distant friend to come near to him, then he begs his Innermost as follows: "My Father, I beg you to bring near to me (name the person), but not as I will, but as you will."

If his Innermost considers that his petition is just, then the Innermost performs the miracle; that is to say, He performs a work of Theurgy, and the distant friend arrives. Yet, if the Innermost considers that the petition is unjust, then the Innermost does not perform the petition of his soul. This is pure White Magic.

The black magician proceeds to use his so called "Asuncion" or willpower without taking the will of his Innermost into account.

"Thy will be done on earth as it is in heaven" is what the Gnostic says, because the Gnostic only performs the will of his Innermost on earth as it is in heaven, in other words, in the superior planes of consciousness. The Gnostic places all of his longings in the hands of his Innermost.

We prepare our pituitary and pineal glands for clairvoyance by dominating anger and acquiring serenity. We prepare ourselves for the awakening of the inner ear when we always utter words of love and truth.

Sexual Magic, daily vocalization, and incessant purification take us towards the summits of the High Initiation.

To not covet powers does not signify that we, the Gnostics, take on a passive attitude, as do the Theosophists. We have to prepare ourselves when practicing Sexual Magic, when vocalizing, and when we expel all of the rubbish from ourselves.

The Gnostics transmute their sexual secretions and wait patiently in order to be worthy of receiving the occult powers that sprout as flowers of the soul it is purified.

The Gnostics do not covet powers, on the contrary, they prepare themselves in order to acquire them. The preparation of the Gnostic is to purify himself and to practice Sexual Magic daily.

In their temples, the black magicians have established similar ordeals to those of the white magicians. In order to be accepted as candidates for their initiation, the likely candidates are made to receive insults, grumbles, to listen to humiliations, and to even receive blows to their person whilst in their festivities.

In the fifth monograph of the ninth black degree of the school of Sodom, the disciple receives a parchment after passing the four ordeals of earth, water, fire, and air within a temple of black magic. The parchment states the following:

> "Peace, greetings from the Master of the temple. By decree of the high priest, and by all of the guardians who have served and veiled over you, as proof of your perseverance, faith and desire, and in accordance with what has been manifested in the external chambers, you are allowed to enter into the following Sanctum. You will await to be prepared in order to be admitted into the holy of holies after three days of sanctification and purification. Your name will be 777, your letter will be R, your salutation will be Aum, your book will be the one with the letter 'M', your jewel will be the green Jasper which is in the shape of a scarab, and your hour will be nine. Rest with patience and await the hour, the number and the sign."

This is pure and legitimate black magic. These ordeals are passed by the disciple in the Astral plane within a temple of black magic.

In the White Lodge, when the Gnostic asks the Masters in the Astral plane for the four ordeals of earth, fire, water, and air, then these ordeals are set by the Masters one after the other (as described in our book *The Perfect Matrimony or the Door to Enter into Initiation*). These ordeals are always occurring with the interruption of many days between each one, and the next ordeal is given only if the student has been triumphant in the previous one.

Each triumph of the disciple is celebrated in the Children's Hall with ineffable music and feasts. Each one of the four ordeals has its special celebration. The Children's Hall is so named because the disciple is received by the Masters who have taken on the shape of children, in order to tell him:

> *Except ye be converted, and become as little children, ye shall not enter into the kingdom of heaven.*   MATTHEW 18:3

So, there is nothing regarding a letter R, nothing about 777, nothing about Jasper jewels, nothing about hours and signs, since all of these are just pure black magic from Atlantis.

In the White Lodge, the only thing which is placed on the Gnostic disciple is the small cape of a chela (neophyte), for which he has to ask.

After having passed the ordeal of air, the black magician receives a jewel with two intertwined rings, which is what becomes the sign of his triumph.

The white magician receives a symbolic ring, which represents the Ray to which he belongs.

The ring of the black magician reminds him that he was hung from two rings over an abyss. The masters of the black temple dress in white tunics. The veiled prophets wear black veils, the stole bearers wear grey colored stoles, the scribes wear blue, the astrologers wear blue and white, the mystics wear yellow, and the doctors wear a reddish-grey colored stole. The temple remains in obscurity.

The disciple of the ninth black degree is admonished with the following words: "The living soul who traverses this horrendous path in loneliness without vacillations or shyness will be illuminated by the glorious mysteries after the purifications by earth, fire, water, and air." Afterwards, the black disciple advances towards the guardians of death.

In the ordeal of fire, a guardian says to the black disciple the following: "If you wish to arrive next to the master, you must pass through this door. In order to reach this door, you must pass through this hall. In order to pass through this hall, you must walk over these beams of fire. So come if you search for the master." Then the disciple says, "Go ahead! Go ahead! Go ahead!" So, filled with courage, he traverses through the fire.

In the ordeal of water, a black guardian says: "If you want to see the master and to enter into the holy temple, you must reach that door and pass through it, and in order to pass that door, you must pass through the lake."

Everything here described between quotations refers to the ninth black degree of the fraternity from the school of Sodom. Everything is pure and legitimate black magic.

The disciples of the White Lodge, as we have already stated, only celebrate their festivity in the Children's Hall after having become triumphant.

The four ordeals within the White Lodge are in order to examine the white disciple's morals. For instance, in the ordeal of fire, the disciple is attacked by crowds of enemies who insult him. Instead of returning insults, the disciple throws love towards his enemies. This is how he triumphs in this ordeal, when with serenity, he passes through the fire without becoming burned.

As we see in this ordeal of fire, there is the need to kiss the executioner's whip in order to triumph. Yet, in the ordeal of fire for the black magician, the only requirement is to pass through the fire, since moral preparation does not have the least bit of importance for the black magician.

The ordeal of water for the Gnostic in the White Lodge is given with the sole purpose of knowing what level the disciple's altruism and philanthropy has reached.

The White Lodge's ordeal of air is given with the sole purpose of knowing the disciple's capacity for resistance against great adversities, and for detachment from material things.

It is logical that a disciple who commits suicide because of a loss of fortune cannot pass through the ordeal of air. By simply not being capable of morally resisting a failure, it is clear that one does not pass the ordeal of air.

The Four Ordeals
BY MICHAEL MAIER,
CA. 1618

Whosoever succumbs to the grave inconveniences of life fails in the ordeal of earth.

There are many persons who have passed these ordeals within the very struggle of life, within the daily battle of obtaining their daily bread.

Sometimes in life there have been human beings who have traced a great plan for the benefit of humanity, and they have accomplished it with exact fullness, in spite of all misfortunes, sufferings, and tears. These people have passed the four ordeals in the body of flesh and bones.

Therefore, the four ordeals of earth, fire, water, and air are presented simply for the moral examination of the disciple. All of our defects and moral faults are precisely the negative aspects of the four elements of Nature, and we have to convert ourselves into kings and queens of it.

In the White Lodge, the four ordeals are accompanied by a verbal test in order to know what level of purification the disciple has reached.

All of these ordeals occur in the Astral plane. The prepared disciple, that is to say, the disciple who has spiritual maturity, brings the memory of all of this to the physical plane, just as if he would have had a dream.

On the other hand, in order to become triumphant in the ordeals the only thing that matters in the Black Lodge is to have the courage of a brutal beast.

The sixth monograph from the ninth black degree describes to us how their dreadful disciples, after having triumphantly passed their four ordeals, have the right to receive (they say) the sacred initiation.

Let us see the following paragraph from the third page of the sixth monograph of the ninth black degree:

> "Now then, in this way I knew that two intertwined rings must be my sign; therefore, two intertwined circles similar to two links of a chain are my sign, and also these will be your sign in this initiation. As soon as this was understood by me, they asked me to sign my name and to leave the digital mark of my thumb over a sheet of special paper, which was attached to a piece of wood, that also was attached to other pieces. Then after, they commanded me to go towards the door, to push a small sliding seal and give my letter and number."

The whole of this seems to be like a scene in a police office, but never of a temple of white initiation. No one signs his personal name within any temple of white initiation, neither is anyone registered because in the White Lodges and in the karmic records, the human being is depicted with the name of his Innermost and never with profane names.

Many of the black students lose their profane name when they enroll in their spiritual universities. Then, when they conquer their "Anagaric-hood," they are assigned a capricious name as a substitution of their own profane name as a reward for their success.

While forming a chain, they exclaim in their Sanctum: "E........... I.......... E.......... I............ E.............. I.............." This is an action of thanksgiving for these left-hand adepts.

The disciple's conductor wears a tunic and hood of a black color because he is an authentic black magician. Among the masters of the White Lodge, not one wears a black hood. The Master Zanoni (white master), dresses in a black tunic and wears a distinguished mantle of the same color, but never a black hood. This is because the black hood is only for black magicians.

> "Thus, having again reached the bottom of the temple, I am lead towards the center of the temple. Then, an official places a great

cross over my head while I kneel, and three bellstrokes resound in some other part of the temple. From the east of the temple, a master with a purple tunic who carries a great Egyptian cross approaches me. He holds this cross over my head instead of the other cross, while other officials who are standing next to me say: 'Under the cross of immortality and eternal life, you are blessed.'"

Within the halls of the authentic White Gnostic Initiation, a master never wears a purple or red tunic since these colors are only used by the hierarchies of the Black Lodge.

In the White Initiation, the disciple throws upon his shoulders an enormous and heavy cross of wood. This signifies that the disciple has already started his own Via Crucis through the nine Arcades. The weight of the cross differs very much as this weight depends upon the karma of each person. Sometimes the disciple cannot bear the weight of his cross, then the Cyrenean has to help him. The vowels **E. U.** grant the disciple the power of bearing his cross when it is very heavy. Thus, the cross over the shoulders is White Magic. Yet, the cross over the head is black magic.

Christ did not bear his cross over his head, but over his shoulders. The cross symbolizes matter. Hence, to bear the cross over the head signifies to resolve oneself to live under matter, under the world. This is why the black magician says: "Under the cross of immortality and eternal life, you are blessed."

The White Magician says: "Over the cross I am." The cross over the head is carried by the Pontiffs on their miters. No White Magician carries the cross over his head, but over his shoulders, as was demonstrated by the Divine Redeemer. Thus, we, the Gnostics, are not under the cross but over the cross.

The Gnostic has to bite a certain figure in the first Initiation. Before entering into this first Initiation, he has already received the authentic lost word, which has never been written.

The verbal tests are very strict in order to receive the Initiation. The black magician does not care for morality.

Once the chela (white neophyte) triumphantly passes the white Initiation, a celebration occurs.

In the black ceremony, the disciple receives from a black magician, who is dressed in yellow, a series of teachings that are utilized in order to become invisible and to make others invisible. We will talk about this in the next chapter, "Nirvana."

As we have already stated, all of these teachings came from Atlantis. In Atlantis, the human beings utilized the sexual force in order to inflict grave damage. This is how Orhuarpa (a black magician) formed monsters with his mind that later he physically materialized. He fed them blood to keep them alive, and he cast these monsters upon his defenseless victims whenever he wished to do so.

The Atlantean humanity was clairvoyant and they marvelously managed to handle the cosmic forces. A very important sanctuary existed in that epoch. This sanctuary was named the Sanctuary of Vulcan. The guardians of this sanctuary had Ariman (another black magician) and his legions under their control so these black magicians could not freely work on our planet. The atoms of Ariman eventually damaged the clairvoyance of the human being. This is how our humanity remains enslaved by the illusion of this physical world.

Nevertheless, there was in Atlantis a great College of Initiates. When the black magicians attempted damage against them, the evil ones were killed by the Sword of Justice.

The Lords of Mercury gave the mind to the human being in order for him to think, and not for him to use it for destructive purposes, as did Orhuarpa.

When Orhuarpa saw that people were worshipping him as a God, he amassed a powerful army and marched against Tollan, the city of the seven gates of massive gold, where the White Magicians from Atlantis reigned.

During the day, Orhuarpa fought dressed in steel with shield, helmet, cask, and sword. Yet, during the night, he unleashed his beasts with his witchcraft. They were in the form of wolves, and they destroyed his enemies. This is how he captured Tollan, the city with the seven gates of massive gold. He became emperor of Atlantis, thus establishing the cult of the tenebrous sun.

This is how events occurred. Then, the Master Moria reincarnated. He reunited an army of soldiers and marched against Orhuarpa.

During the day, Orhuarpa fought dressed in steel with shield, helmet, cask and sword. Yet, during the night, he unleashed his beasts with his witchcraft.

ENGRAVING BY GUSTAVE DORÉ

Orhuarpa cast his ferocious beasts against the Master Moria, but the Master dissolved them with his luminous powers.

Master Moria, with the edge of his sword, captured Tollan, the city with the seven gates of massive gold, and all of the soldiers of Orhuarpa fell under the sword of the forces of light.

When Orhuarpa saw that he had lost, he enclosed himself within a tower and died burning in it, because Master Moria's soldiers set fire to that tower.

Unfortunately, events did not end here. Orhuarpa immediately reincarnated again, and when he was old enough, he reunited his army of warriors and sorcerers and marched against Tollan, but he could not capture the city again. So, he established his own throne against the other throne.

Then, the Four Thrones (Deities) said to the White Emperor Noenra (Noah), "Leave from this land, and pass to the Gobi desert, where you will find dry land, because God will sink this land." Noah obeyed and departed with all his people towards the Gobi desert.

The people of Noenra were the primitive Semite tribes who were following the path of White Magic. Thus, Orhuarpa remained chief and lord of Atlantis.

Sometime after the departure of the people of Israel, certain dangerous igneous manifestations started to appear in Atlantis. This was because the use of the sexual forces, when utilized for black magic, made the fire of the dormant volcanoes enter into activity.

The sexual forces have an intimate relationship with all the forces of Nature, because the sexual forces reside not only in our sexual organs, but also in all of our cells, and moreover, within each atom of the Cosmos.

The sexual force is the cause of electricity. It is logical then that the dormant volcanoes would enter into activity, since the volcanoes were intimately related with the black magicians by means of the sexual energy.

During great earthquakes, Atlantis sank with all of its black magicians into the bottom of the Atlantic Ocean.

All of the native tribes from the continent of America are Atlantean remnants. These tribes preserved many practices of black magic which were derived from the Atlanteans.

In America, there are some who make dolls with wax and then bury them with pins. This is how they empower their imagination and concentrate their minds on their victims.

There are others who utilize the sexual forces with destructive purposes. The whole of this originated in Atlantis.

The Arhuaco Indians, from the Sierra Nevada of Santa Marta, Colombia, burned a whole town named Dibuya by utilizing the elementals of fire which they call "Animes."

I met a humble old woman in the small town of Santa Cruz de Mora (State of Merida), who made marvels with the elementals of nature. When she was young, she married an Indian. Her husband took her to his tribe into the jungle. She tells many strange things about this tribe. She says that during the day, the Indians abandon their homes and during the night all of them arrive with the shape of animals; yet, when they are within their huts, they take the human shape again.

A certain day her husband took leave from her and said that he was going to die in the jungle (since these Indians go into the jungle in order to die). He gave her an amulet and said: "I deliver this keepsake to you, so you can ask of it whatever you wish when you are needy."

This is how the old woman made marvels in the town of Santa Cruz. She asked this amulet whatever she wished for. Money, wine, jewels, liquors, perfumes, etc. were coming to her as if by magic.

People who were robbed did nothing more but consult her. At once she asked the amulet for the robbed object. Then, the object was carried by invisible hands and arrived into her hands, and so everybody recovered their lost things.

Unfortunately, these marvels ended for the old woman when she had the weakness of confessing this to a priest who took this marvelous talisman away from her.

The performance of these marvels are nothing fantastic or rare since they are simply made with the elementals of Nature. The book by Mr. Franz Hartmann entitled *The Elementals* widely refers to these things.

The whole of this knowledge comes from Atlantis.

The elementals serve for good as well as for evil. The Atlanteans utilized the elementals for evil.

ENGRAVING BY GUSTAVE DORÉ

CHAPTER 15

Nirvana

From the Gobi desert, the Israelite tribes emigrated to the west in order to form the Aryan Root Race. This is represented in the Book of Exodus in the story of the emigration of Israel from the land of Egypt towards the Promised Land.

Enormous caravans of human beings who were commanded by the Masters of Major Mysteries came away from the drowning Atlantis towards the Gobi desert. Afterwards, they emigrated to the west in order to cross themselves with some western races in order to form our present Aryan Root Race.

The captains of the Biblical Exodus were the same Masters of Major Mysteries. They were profoundly venerated by humanity; therefore, no one dared to disobey their sacred commands.

Moses remained forty years in the wilderness, that is to say, the primeval Israelites remained forty years in the wilderness. They built the Ark of Alliance, established the mysteries of Levi, and worshipped Jehovah.

The mysteries of the seven sanctuaries emigrated towards the west. Under the light of these sanctuaries the Magi's Persia, the Richi's India, Chaldea, Egypt, Hellenic Greece, etc., all flourished.

This occult wisdom illuminated Solon, Pythagoras, Heraclitus, Socrates, Plato, Aristotle, Buddha, etc.

The most powerful civilizations from the past flourished under the light of the sacred mysteries.

Nonetheless, the human being developed the intellect and it withdrew him from the internal worlds. When the human being lost his clairvoyance, then he knew fear. Fear did not exist in the past, because the human being contemplated the action of the Gods, and he saw the unraveling of all things.

The human being removed himself from the Great Light; now he has to return into the Great Light.

The Buddhists tell us that when the human being is liberated from the wheel of birth and death, then he enters into the ineffable joy of Nirvana.

We, the Gnostics, know that Christ is a Nirmanakaya, a Being who renounced Nirvana in order to come save this humanity.

The Book of the Dead says:

> I am the sacred crocodile Sebek. I am the flame with three wicks, and my wicks are immortal. I enter the region of Sekem; I enter into the region of the flames, which have defeated my adversaries.

This region of Sekem, the region of the flames, is the ineffable joy of Nirvana.

A Dhyan-Chohan is one who has already abandoned the four bodies of sin, which are the physical, Astral, Mental, and Causal Bodies.

A Dhyan-Chohan only acts with his Diamond Soul. He has already liberated himself from Maya (illusion); thus, he lives happily in Nirvana.

The sacred crocodile is the Innermost. The Innermost is the flame with three immortal wicks. These three wicks are the Innermost's Diamond Soul, his Igneous Mind and Atman, his own spiritual body.

Nirvana is a region of Nature where the ineffable happiness of the fire reigns. The Nirvanic plane has seven sub-planes. A resplendent hall exists in each one of these seven sub-planes of Nirvanic matter where the Nirmanakayas study their mysteries. This is why they call their sub-planes "halls" and not merely "sub-planes" as the Theosophists do.

The Nirvanis say, "We are in the first hall of Nirvana or in the second hall of Nirvana, or in the third, or in the fourth, or fifth, or sixth, or in the seventh hall of Nirvana."

To describe the ineffable joy of Nirvana is impossible. There, the music of the spheres reigns and the soul is enchanted within a state of bliss, which is impossible to describe with words.

The inhabitants of the superior hall of Nirvana use diamond tunics, and over their heads carry mantles of distinction that fall to their feet.

We can visit Nirvana with our Astral Body. The yogis from India, while in the state of Samadhi, visit Nirvana with their

Mental Body or Causal Body. However, to pretend to visit Nirvana with black magic procedures is the breaking point of madness.

The Gnostic knows how to enter into Nirvana by utilizing the powers of his Innermost. When the Gnostic wants to visit Nirvana, he does the following:

First, he leaves his physical body and departs in his Astral Body.

Second, when he is already out of his physical body, then he prays to his Innermost as follows: "Father of mine, take me to Nirvana." Then, the Innermost transports the soul of the Gnostic towards the ineffable joys of Nirvana.

The Gnostic procedure in order to depart in the Astral Body is very simple.

The Gnostic takes advantage of the natural state of transition between vigil and dream in order to leave his physical body. This is done naturally, as when one is walking out of his home. The individual simply pronounces the mantra **RUSTI,** and in the moment when he is getting drowsy, he gets out of his bed - not with the mind, nor the imagination, but as if he is really doing it with his body of flesh and bones. Hence, the physical body remains within the bed. The mantra is pronounced many times like this: *Rrruuusssssssssssssssssttiiiiiiiiiiiiiiiiiiiiii.*

The Gnostics know very well that they must always save their sexual force, because the Kundalini awakens with the sexual force.

The mantra **RA** helps in the awakening of the Kundalini, but it is necessary to know how. This is ignored by the black magicians of the school of Sodom. These black magicians believe that by pronouncing "RA-MA" while standing on their feet every morning and while taking various inhalations of air, they will purify themselves. The only thing they demonstrate with this is their complete ignorance regarding the wisdom of the Egyptians.

We, the ancient Egyptians, pronounce the mantra **RA** while in the Egyptian position which is as follows: Our knees are on the ground, the palms of our hands are on the ground and touching each other by the thumbs. Then, our head rests upon the back of our hands. In this position, one pronounces many times the mantra like this: *RrrrrrrrrAaaaaaaaaaa.*

ENGRAVING BY GUSTAVE DORÉ

As we have already stated (in the previous chapter), in the black ceremony, the ancient black magicians, while enveloped within a cloud, were physically invisible and transported themselves to wherever they wished.

Christ, the divine Rabbi of Galilee, taught us the secret in order to travel with the physical body within the Astral plane. Let us see verses 24-32 of the fourteenth chapter of Matthew.

> But the ship was now in the midst of the sea, tossed with waves: for the wind was contrary. And in the fourth watch of the night Jesus went unto them, walking on the sea. And when the disciples saw him walking on the sea, they were troubled, saying, It is a spirit; and they cried out for fear. But, straightway Jesus spake unto them saying, Be of good cheer; It is I; be not afraid. And Peter answered him and said, Lord if it be thou, bid me come unto thee on the water. And he said, Come. And when Peter was come down out of the ship, he walked on the water, to go to Jesus. But when he saw the wind boisterous, he was afraid; and beginning to sink, he cried, saying, Lord save me. And immediately Jesus stretched forth his hand, and caught him, and said unto him, O thou of little faith, wherefore didst thou doubt? And when they were come into the ship, the wind ceased.

This is the Gnostic secret in order to enter within the Astral plane with the body of flesh and bones.

Peter walked upon the waters because his physical body, by means of the force of faith, submerged itself within the Astral plane. In the moment when he doubted, he went out of the Astral plane, and he was close to sinking.

The forces of the Astral plane held Peter when he was upon the waters. Therefore, the Astral plane was the force which held Christ when he was upon the waters.

When we, the Gnostics, want to go to the Astral plane with the body of flesh and bones, we then utilize the clue that the Master taught us.

We proceed in the following way: In the precise moment when we awaken from our natural sleep, without giving time to any analysis, doubt, or vacillation, and filled with a very intense faith, we get up from our bed, we leave our room, and float within the atmosphere.

Faith alone is what holds us while performing this exercise. Consequently, any analysis, doubt, or vacillation damages the experiment.

We can also take advantage of the instant in which we are getting sleepy, or simply the instant in which the mind is in a profound repose, as a tranquil lake.

The physical body floats simply by means of faith. We abandon the force of gravity and the physical plane. So, we penetrate with our physical body into the Astral plane where the laws of levitation reign.

Our disciples know how to walk upon the waters in the same way as our Master did. Therefore, we are authentic Christians.

The black magicians from the school of Sodom also utilize the procedure of the cloud in order to envelop themselves within it and become invisible. They do not forget about "mimicry" with this, since, if they are within a jungle, they have to make the cloud green; if they are within a room of white walls, they have to make the cloud white. In this way they will become invisible.

We, the White Magicians, utilize the power of our Innermost in order to become invisible; yet, this power is delivered to us only when we deserve it.

The black magicians from the school of Sodom believe that with their black experiments they can penetrate into Nirvana; yet, they are mistaken. They penetrate into the Astral plane, but not into Nirvana.

We, the Gnostics, can visit Nirvana even with our body of flesh and bones. Obviously, modern Theosophists will laugh at us because they know naught about these things. The unique thing that they have in their heads is an arsenal of theories. But in practicality, they are nothing but eunuchs of understanding, morbid mystics, and fornicating sybarites.

I still remember a Theosophist who was a member of a Black Lodge. How terrified he flew away from a park in Cartagena (South America) when I told him that he was consciously working in the Astral plane.

This is the breaking point of negativity from Theosophists. They horrify themselves simply with thinking of awakening the consciousness. They are only interested in having their heads filled with "cockroaches" and in living their life asleep. Nevertheless, they say that some day they think they will enter Nirvana.

Foolish boasters of wisdom, know that only those who have already passed through the High Initiation, only those who have given their last drop of blood for this humanity, will enter into Nirvana.

All men long for the High Initiation; yet, they can only reach the altar of the High Initiation with the virile member in the state of erection (explanation in next chapter).

Therefore, the Gnostic always lives heroically, always triumphant and always a rebel, like the heroes of Rabelais, who knew nothing of weakness.

The Gnostics yearn for Nirvana, but they know very well that they carry Nirvana within their sexual glands. Thus, they want to Self-realize it within themselves by means of courage.

CHAPTER 16
The Elixir of Long Life

The Master Zanoni acquired his Chaldean Initiation in very remote ages. As a result, he preserved his youthfulness for thousands of years. Megnour, who was Zanoni's comrade, also lived through entire ages. These masters were invincible; death could not do anything against them. They were citizens of an already-vanished ancient nation (Chaldea). What was their secret? What was their power?

When arriving at the present chapter of this book, many uneducated surgeons of occult medicine will look at us with condemnation. With compassionate gestures they will mock the "Elixir of Long Life" and will consider these teachings senseless, since they feel they are something impossible for them.

People have never comprehended, neither have they wanted to admit, that the Elixir of Long Life, the Philosophical Stone, and the Clue of Perpetual Movement are found within the male testicles and within the female uterus.

We have already said, and we will not tire of repeating, that Initiation is life itself, intensively lived, and that the human being's redemption lies exclusively in the sexual act.

When our book *The Perfect Matrimony* started to circulate, then, as we had expected, many critics emerged who qualified us as pornographic. This was because the book was written in a simple language which was at the reach of everyone's comprehension, and also because the clue of Sexual Magic was given.

Nonetheless, we know that for the pure ones, everything is pure; yet, for the impure ones, everything is impure.

This is how the "boasters of wisdom," the sick mystics, who through their morbid lucubrations (which make them believe that they are super-transcended) came to qualify us as materialists.

Such individuals totally ignore that nothing can exist, not even God, without the help of matter.

Some old rascals, filled with decrepitude and consumed by the passionate coitus, and some sanctimonious, sexually unsatisfied

Men were made for women and women for men because
Nature is wise in its designs. What man and woman have to
learn is to enjoy themselves without hurting each other, and the
answer for this is 'sexual magic.'

old women, threw the book away horrified, and qualified it as scandalous and pornographic. This is because humanity does not love good, but only evil.

There were also some hallucinated mystics who pleaded in favor of an absurd type of chastity, which some religious sects preach, but do not practice. They ignore that Nature is in rebellion against that harmful abstinence, which causes nocturnal pollutions and the decalcification of the organism through the urethra. Sickness is the consequence.

Men were made for women and women for men, because Nature is wise in its designs. What man and woman have to learn is to enjoy themselves without hurting each other, and the answer for this is Sexual Magic.

During the act of love, the Gnostic couple transmutes their semen into atomic energy by restraining the sexual act. This energy then rises upwards towards their head, through certain spermatic canals. This is how the human being is converted into a God.

This is not understood, cannot be understood, neither can it be explained by the pseudo-apostles of modern medicine, simply because they do not know the anatomy of the seven bodies of the human being.

They do not know about the occult chemistry or the ultra-biology of the interior organisms of the human being which are the fundamental base of the hormonal life and of the endocrine glands.

The Hindus gave the name "Ida and Pingala" to the spermatic canals through which the sexual energy internally rises towards the head. These are nervous cords, which are related with the Vagus and Sympathetic systems. These cords are entwined along the spinal column in the symbolic shape represented by the Caduceus of Mercury.

The human organism has its canals for the spilling of the semen. However, it also possesses seminal canals through which the semen, when transformed into energy, rises from the seminal glands upwards towards the head. This is because the mass (semen) is always transformed into energy, as was already proven by the wise and great Einstein. This process is what we call "transmutation."

These ascending spermatic canals were in use by human beings in very ancient epochs. The doctors of medicine among the Indians of the Sierra Nevada from Santa Marta (Colombia) have utilized these canals since very ancient times. This is why they reach a very old age, maintaining a very lucid understanding, black hair, and intact dentures.

Among these Indians, we frequently see their children reach the octogenarian and centenarian ages, while in our present civilization, the human being is already in decrepitude by the age of seventy.

There exist thousands of examples of this kind of evidence in order to make the civilized and scientific person to think upon this particular matter.

For example, an infant whose sexual energy has not yet been collected in his gonads has this energy latent in all of his organism. This is why if this infant is wounded, his body will heal more rapidly than the body of an adult, because the adult has been wasting his sexual forces since puberty. Moreover, the adult does not know how to handle his sexual energies as in the case of the infant.

Great is the error which the youth commit and also which their parents commit when they allow their children to squander the sexual force in pleasures and disgusting habits. They need to be taught that the vital principle resides within this great force.

It is true, as official science states, that sex is a biological function. Yet, the Decalogue teaches us with its sixth commandment that we must not squander the sexual force, because this force should only accomplish a constructive or creative function.

Therefore, the liberty which the parents give to their children, in order for them to freely fulfill their biological functions, is not short of being a crime committed against the youth.

Sexual Magic has the following advantages:

1. Husband and wife continue loving each other for life with growing intensity, as if they were boyfriend and girlfriend.

2. It does not fill the spouses' lives with children.

3. Woman rejuvenates, she turns more beautiful and attractive every day, because she is daily charged with powerful forces, thanks to her husband.

4. Aged man rejuvenates and does not ever get old, because life is given to him through their creative forces. Thus, luck and happiness surround them everywhere.

5. The sense of clairvoyance is awakened in both, and so the veil of the invisible worlds is disclosed before their sight.

6. The sacred fire of the Holy Spirit illuminates them internally.

7. They unite themselves with their own Innermost (internal God). Thus, they convert themselves into king and queen of creation, with powers over the four elements of Nature: earth, water, air and fire.

8. They acquire the Elixir of Long Life, which resides in the Kundalini.

9. Death will be no more.

All of this is a fact, in spite of the doctors, who are "consecrated" by materialistic universities.

Heaven is taken by assault, because heaven is for the courageous ones.

The Gnostics, protected with their character-shield of steel, grasp their sword of will, and as terrific warriors, they hurl themselves into battle in order to take heaven by assault.

We, the Gnostics, are human beings of great tempests, and within the explosion of thunder, we understand only the language of majesty.

When the warrior is close to the Initiation, then he can laugh at death with a guffaw that can shake all of the caverns of the earth. Then, he can have the right to the Elixir of Long Life, which is a potable gold, and a liquid, flexible, and malleable glass. He asks the Lords of Karma for additional years of life in order to pay his debts.

This is how death and resurrection are achieved in his present incarnation and how he is united with his Innermost. Then, when his own karma is paid, he convokes the Lords of Karma in order to declare to them that he has resolved to remain in this world in order to work for humanity. Therefore, he remains with his physical body forever, till the end of all centuries.

The Masters Kout Humi, Moria, Saint Germain, etc. have physical bodies which have existed for thousands of years. All of them have an indescribable age. What would a Master of Major Mysteries do if he had to constantly change his physical body?

The founder of the College of Initiates is a Maha-Guru, who will remain with us until the last Initiate has reached his rank.

The author of *The Dayspring of Youth* tells us that in Egypt there exist two Masters who have a really indescribable age. He states that one of them is mentioned within very ancient religious scriptures.

A Master can preserve his physical body for millions of years because he possesses the Elixir of Long Life, which resides in the Kundalini. The Master engenders his own body daily, by means of his Kundalini. Thus, the cells of the body of a Master never wither, because the fire of the Kundalini does not allow them to do so.

The Kundalini is then the Elixir of Long Life. This fire is the potable gold of ancient Alchemists. The Kundalini is the Tree of Life, which the book of Genesis refers to in the following verses:

> And of the ground made Jehovah Elohim to grow every tree that is pleasant to the sight, and good for food; the tree of life also in the midst of the garden, and the tree of knowledge of good and evil.
> Genesis 2:9

The Tree of Life is the Kundalini and the Tree of Knowledge of Good and Evil is the semen. Both trees are from the garden of God.

> And a river went out of Eden to water the garden; and from thence it was parted, and became into four heads.
>
> The name of the first is Pison: that is it which compasseth the whole land of Havilah, where there is gold; and the gold of that land is good: there is bdellium and the onyx stone.

The land of Havilah is our own physical body, and the gold of this land is the solar atoms from our seminal system, that is to say, the semen's potable gold.

And the name of the second river is Gihon: the same is it that compasseth the whole land of Ethiopia.

This second river is the Cephalo-Rachis liquid, which is the other pole of our seminal system. With it we encompass the whole land of Ethiopia, that is to say, the whole of our head and throat, since we form the brain and throat with the Cephalo-Rachis liquid.

And the name of the third river is Hiddekel: that is it which goeth toward the east of Assyria. And the fourth river is Euphrates.
Genesis 2:10-14

The river which goes toward the east of Assyria and the river Euphrates are the two poles of the woman's seminal system. Therefore, the woman is towards the east of us, because she is the door of Paradise and this door is always towards the east.

Eden is sex itself. Thus, the Tree of Life is within Eden itself. The great Hierophant Eliphas Levi said that the Great Magical Arcanum is the Tree of Life and that "at the foot of this Tree is the source of the four mysterious rivers of Eden." Yet, he fearfully says in a moment of consternation: "Here I must pause, and I fear that already I have said too much."

This is the formidable, unutterable secret which no Initiate has ever dared to reveal. This is the formidable secret of the "Great Arcanum."

The four rivers of Eden are the sexual forces of man and woman. The Tree of Life is in the midst of these four rivers of Eden.

If the human being, with all of his vices and passions, could have eaten from the Tree of Life in Eden, then Nero still would be alive, and the great tyrants would not have left a single moment of light for humanity. Caligula and the twelve Caesars from Rome would still be alive, they would still be upon their thrones. Fortunately, Jehovah knew how to keep the way of the Tree of Life.

So, he drove out the man: and he placed at the east of the garden of Eden a cherubim, and a flaming sword which turned every way, to keep the way of the tree of life. Genesis 3:24

Ignite your nine mystic lamps, oh chela!

Listen to me, a Master abides in the bottom of your soul; he awaits in mystical lurking, waiting for the hour that He will be Self-realized.

Listen to me, beloved disciple: that Master is your Innermost and you are the soul of that Master.

The Innermost becomes Master with the fruits of millinery experiences through innumerable reincarnations.

Do not forget, beloved disciple, that you are a soul and that your physical body is your suit.

Listen to me, beloved disciple: When your outfit is damaged, what do you do with it? You throw it away, because you no longer need it, and you cannot deny this. Yet, if you wish to replace your outfit, then where do you go? You might answer me that you will go to the tailor's store in order for the tailor to make another outfit for you.

Therefore, beloved disciple, I have already told you that you are a soul and that your body is your suit. Your suit of flesh was well-made in accordance to your own proportions. This suit of flesh was made by two laborers, that is to say, your father and your mother.

When your present suit of flesh is damaged, what will you do with it? You will throw it from you, and if you want to replace it, then you have to search for a new pair of male and female laborers in order for them to build for you another suit of flesh, well-made and in accordance to your own proportions.

You might ask me how? Well, how was your present suit of flesh which you use made? In the same way, the new tailors will make for you your new suit. So then, this should not be strange to you.

When you undress yourself, taking off your fabric clothing, and you put on another garment, it is clear that you do not stop being Mr. or Ms. X. Neither do you forget your business and your debts. So, whether wearing a suit of cotton or wearing another of wool, you will always pay your debts.

The same happens when you, as a soul, re-dress yourself with a new suit of flesh. You have to pay your old debts, and you have to pay them because there is no other way, since these debts are your evil actions.

Listen to me, beloved reader. There are millions of suits of flesh which you have taken off since the beginning of the world. If you do not remember, indeed other people do remember. A day will come in which you will remember your millions of deaths and births from the very constitution of the world.

Do not forget that Adam is not one man, neither is Eve one woman. Indeed, Adam is all of the millions of men of Lemuria, and Eve is all of the millions of women of Lemuria.

The souls that in this day and age you see wearing a suit of flesh and bones are the same souls of Lemuria, who in those times were wearing other suits of flesh and bones.

In the dawn of life, the Four Thrones emanated from their own life source millions of human bodies in an embryonic state. These human bodies were developed through the ages. Now they are our marvelous physical bodies, which are made from the mud of the earth.

All of this is explained by the Bible. Yet, in order to study the Bible, one needs to have studied occultism, because the Bible is a book of occultism and cannot be read at face value as when reading a newspaper.

Therefore, the Bible is the book of the Gnostics, and only when one becomes a Gnostic can one understand it.

The Mystery of Life and Death

Listen, dear reader, each time that you wear a new suit of flesh, you are a little less of a villain, a little less of an assassin, a little less envious. This is because one truly learns from life's club blows, and the soul is really perfected through suffering. When the wild colt is tamed with a whip, then the day for the soul to be united with its Innermost arrives, and the soul is converted into an angel.

This is performed through being born and through dying millions of times; yet, it is also very true that we can achieve the union with the Innermost in just one very well spent life.

It is also very true that we can preserve our youth and not die by means of the Elixir of Long Life.

Megnour lived with his body of flesh and bones for seven times seven centuries. Zanoni also remained young for millions of years.

The Count Saint Germain presently lives in Tibet with the same body that he had during the XVII, XVIII, and part of the XIX centuries in Europe.

We, the Gnostics, laugh at death. We have the secret in order to mock the mute skull, and as we previously stated in the first chapter, we will make the inopportune guest (death) flee with the sword of Damocles.

We feel ourselves omnipotent and with a gesture of sovereign rebellion, we challenge science.

Foolish doctors, ignorant biologists, arrogant physicists, where is your wisdom?

Death sweeps away everyone, wealthy and poor, believers and unbelievers. All are defeated by death, except we, the Gnostics.

We, the Gnostics, laugh at death, and we place it before our feet, because we are omnipotent.

Ignite your nine mystic lamps, oh Lanu (disciple). Remember that each one of the nine Initiations of Minor Mysteries has a musical note and an instrument which produces it.

There are three conditions that are necessary in order to receive the Elixir of Long Life: Sexual Magic, perfect sanctity, and to know how to consciously travel in the Astral Body.

Many people can start by traveling with their own physical body within the Astral plane, because this is easier. Later on, they can become practical in the use and control of the Astral Body.

Some people are acquiring their sanctity little by little. The best way to put it into effect is to make an addition of all of our defects, then to terminate each one of them in a successive order, by dedicating two months to each defect.

Whosoever wants to terminate various defects at one time is similar to the hunter who wants to hunt ten hares at the same time. He does not succeed in hunting any one of them.

Now, concerning Sexual Magic, there is the need to accustom the organism little by little to it, for there exist such brutal individuals who would not feel the slightest bit of pain if their own leg was cut during the sexual act. These are human beasts.

In the beginning, the couple can practice standing on their feet. The husband will massage his wife from the coccyx upwards towards her neck, with his index, middle fingers and his thumb, with the intention of awakening the Kundalini of his wife. She, likewise, will do the same thing to her husband, with the intention of awakening his Kundalini. The mind should be concentrated on the spinal medulla and not in the sexual organs.

The days for beginners of Sexual Magic will be Thursdays and Fridays at dawn. In the beginning, there should be no sexual connection. Later on (days, maybe weeks), the man will introduce his penis within the vagina and opportunely withdraw it in order to avoid the seminal ejaculation.

Man and woman must mutually kiss and caress during this practice, pronouncing the mantra **I.A.O.** like this: *Iiiiiiiiiiiiii Aaaaaaaaaaa Ooooooooooo,* seven or more times, taking an inhalation of air for each letter.

When strong pain is felt in the coccyx, then it is a sign that the fire of Kundalini has awakened. This fire will rise along the canal of the spinal column, canyon by canyon (vertebra by vertebra) in accordance with our moral merits.

The awakening of the Kundalini is celebrated in the Children's Hall with a great celebration.

The decisive factor in the progress, development and evolution of the Kundalini is ethics.

There is the need for the disciple to be skillful in the astral, so that he can assist the Praetor of the Holy Gnostic Church at dawn on Fridays and Sundays. The other days, the disciple can receive wisdom within the Temple's hall of esoteric instruction.

At the gate of the Holy Gnostic Church, there are some guardians who allow the entrance of the disciples based on the condition that their conduct was upright during the day. These guardians have certain scales with which they weigh the good and evil deeds that the disciples performed during the day.

Also, there exists within the Gnostic Church a lens with which the colors of the disciple can be examined. When the disciple does not carry all of his complete colors, then he cannot bring the memories into his body. Many times, due to daily preoccupations, these colors remain within the physical body.

An extremely fine nervous tissue, which is totally unknown by the men of science, exists in our brain. This tissue is the instrument in order for us to bring back our internal memories. Yet, when an injury is present in such a tissue, then the disciple cannot bring back his memories into his brain. Then, there is the need to ask the Masters Hermes, Hippocrates, or Paracelsus for the healing of such a center.

A letter must be written to the Temple of Alden, asking for the help of any of the three mentioned Masters. Such a letter must firstly be saturated with the smoke of frankincense. Afterwards, the letter must be burned with fire, while pronouncing the mantras **Om Tat Sat Om**.

One must perform this action filled with faith, kneeling, praying to heaven and begging to be heard.

Certainly, the material part of the letter is burned; yet, the Astral counterpart goes directly to the hands of the Master to which the letter is meant.

Thus, the Master reads the Astral counterpart of the letter and then proceeds to heal the disciple.

The Temple of Alden is the Temple of Science.

The internal bodies also get sick and are also in need of the assistance of these doctors. These doctors are the Masters of Science, who are wealthy in wisdom. They heal the internal bodies of the Initiates and also of anyone who asks for help.

One of the most grave inconveniences for practicing Sexual Magic is impotence. The excessive performance of the coitus brings, among other things, impotence. None of the remedies which were invented by allopathic doctors have given any cure for this. Yet, the daily practice of Sexual Magic heals impotence.

Now we are going to give a formula in order for those who suffer that terrible sickness (impotence) to be healed, with the condition that there has not been any injury to the virile member.

Very few are the human beings who have stopped to meditate upon the transcendental value of the plant called the Aloe.

I have seen the Aloe plant hung on a wall without pure air, without water, light, and soil. Nonetheless, it remains filled with life; it multiplies its leaves and miraculously reproduces itself. What does it live on? What does it take for nourishment?

This precisely is an inconvenience for the modern pseudo-botanists, since they only duplicate what others say. Very seldom does one of them have the insight to individually investigate within the marvellous laboratory of Nature.

The unique thing which the pharmacists can do with the Aloe is create "German liquor" and pectorals. These are the only things which they make with their famous Aloe gel. It is a great pectoral, yet they do not even remotely know about the transcendental importance of the Aloe.

The Aloe nourishes itself with the ultrasensible rays of the sun with the christonic substance of the sun. The Aloe gel is the crystallization of the Astral Light from the sun. Therefore, the gel is the semen of the Sun. This is why a great similitude exists between the Aloe gel and the human semen.

Consequently, the Aloe is a great panacea for the healing of impotence.

The procedure is as follows: put into a casserole dish, pan or pot one white panela (hard sugarcane commonly found in Colombia) so it can be melted by the fire. This casserole dish must not contain water. Once the panela is liquefied, you must add the gel of a complete Aloe plant, then add ten grams of iron. Stir this very well with a handmill while on the fire. When everything is very well stirred, then take the casserole dish from the fire and bottle up this substance, adding a little bit of sodium benzoate, so that it cannot ferment. Label it, and take one spoonful of the remedy every hour. Impotence is cured with this marvelous formulae.

ALOE

We will give another marvellous formula for the healing of impotence in our next book which is in preparation, entitled *Occult Medicine and Practical Magic*.

Any woman who wants to awaken her Kundalini must practice Sexual Magic with her husband. She must also vocalize the mantra **I.A.O.** and refrain from the orgasm. Thus, the woman must withdraw herself from her husband before the approaching of the spilling of her feminine semen. This is the way in which women can awaken their Kundalini in a positive way.

The unique difference of the female with the male in relation to the Kundalini is that the two ganglionic canals called Ida and Pingala are inverted. In the male, Ida is at his right and Pingala at his left. In the female, Ida is at her left and Pingala at her right. These two ganglionic canals resound with the note **Fa** of Nature.

Listen to me, beloved reader, when you feel that you are well prepared, then ask the Masters in the Holy Gnostic Church to submit you to the rigorous ordeals. If you wish special assistance, then invoke me, Samael Aun Weor. I will guide you through the nine gates which will give you the right to rise to the Golgotha of the High Initiation with the rough and heavy cross which is delivered to you in the first Initiation of Minor Mysteries.

Remember, good disciple, that the cross weighs the weight of your own Karma. Do not allow yourself to fall, because the disciple who allows himself to fall has to suffer and fight very much in order to recuperate the loss.

Listen to me, good disciple, the path is hard and filled with cobblestones and thorns. Poverty and infamy will put on their masks in order to hurt you in the middle of your journey. You will sweat blood and your feet will also bleed in the middle of your journey because of the cobblestones on the path.

The path of High Initiation is the path of Golgotha. It is a path of tears and anguish.

Light your candles in the silence of the night, and in that profound silence where you keep vigil, remember your Internal God and enter into His cavern. He awaits for you inside, deep inside of yourself, awaiting for the hour of His realization.

Light your candle, oh chela! In the silence of the night, penetrate very deeply into the sacred city of the serpent. Here, inside, is where your God is waiting for you. So, light the fire in the night, oh lanu. Close your eyes, withdraw your mind from any type of mundane preoccupations, become a little sleepy and try to talk with your Internal God in mystery through interior meditation.

When through profound interior meditation you learn how to enter within your own cavern, then, oh disciple, you will converse with your own Innermost.

Ignite your sacred fire in the profound night where you keep your vigil; thus, you will leave the dense obscurity. Your God wants to talk to you within the burning bush of Oreb.

Let your chant become sensitive to your seven churches, oh disciple, and do not forget that the Word is what opens the seven doors of the seven churches of your organism. Chant, oh disciple, chant!

Ephesus corresponds to the note DO. Smyrna corresponds to the note RE. Pergamus corresponds to the note MI. Thyatira corresponds to the note FA. Sardis corresponds to the note SOL. Philadelphia corresponds to the note LA. Laodicea corresponds to the musical note TI.

I: Clairvoyance, middlebrow, note TI

E: Occult ear, larynx, note SOL

O: Intuition, heart, note FA

U: Telepathy, solar plexus, note MI

A: Memory of past lives, lungs, note LA

Chanting these vowels for one hour daily awakens all of these occult powers.

Chakra Sahasrara — Church of Laodicea
Chakra Ajna — Church of Philadelphia
Chakra Vishuddha — Church of Sardis
Chakra Anahata — Church of Thyatira
Chakra Manipura — Church of Pergamos
Chakra Swadhisthana — Church of Smyrna
Chakra Muladhara — Church of Ephesus

The blood rises upwards towards the head when we vocalize the vowel I. The blood goes into the throat with the vowel E. With the O it goes into the heart. The blood goes into the intestines with the vowel U and into the lungs with the A.

Within one of the rituals which the Master Huiracocha brought to Colombia, there is a mantric prayer which is useful for Sexual Magic. This prayer must be pronounced in the moment when the husband and his priestess-wife are practicing the connection of Sexual Magic. This prayer is as follows:

Prayer

Oh Hadit, winged serpent of light, be thou the Gnostic secret of my Being, the central point of my connection, my heart itself. The sacred sphere and the blue of the sky are mine:

O A O Kakof Na Khonsa

O A O Kakof Na Khonsa

O A O Kakof Na Khonsa

When the Kundalini lights the atoms of language which are located within the seminal system, then the human being acquires the power of speaking in all of the languages of the world. The great Illuminated ones of the Atlantean chain spoke all of the languages of the world.

The Kundalini becomes a creator in the throat. The Magi can create a figure with his mind and materialize it by means of the creative Word of his Kundalini. This is how the angels create living things.

When the human being is united with his Innermost upon reaching the High Initiation, he then utters the divine golden Word, that the Gods utter. This is how we elevate ourselves to the pleroma of eternal happiness, and how we convert ourselves into creative Gods by means of the Word.

Therefore, a book whose theme is about the Word, yet does not teach Sexual Magic, is simply flippant.

To take the Word out from the mysteries of sex is the breaking point of madness, since sex is the very base of the Word. Thus, one cannot utter the divine golden Word (language) without the awakening of the Kundalini, and Kundalini is only awakened by practicing Sexual Magic.

Whosoever is united with the Innermost becomes omnipotent and omniscient. He knows how to command and to obey; he never becomes arrogant because he has learned to be simple and humble within the cosmos.

The Master's sight penetrates within all of the spheres of Nature. As a Sovereign of the Infinite, he unleashes the tempests and calms the hurricanes. He makes the earth tremble, the lightning serves him as a scepter, and the fire as a carpet for his feet.

We will acquire the Elixir of Long Life by practicing Sexual Magic. Thus, we will become omnipotent. Yet, in order to achieve omnipotence, it is first necessary to learn how to obey the White Hierarchy.

> *I am Alpha and Omega, the beginning and the end, the first and the last.*
>
> *Blessed are they that do his commandments, that they might have right to the tree of life, and may enter in through the gates into the city.* REVELATION 22:13-14

The Song of Songs

I feel within my inner most parts a tormenting fire.
It is the delectable wine of love...
I am the Rose of Sharon,
and the lily of the valleys,
I am the delectable perfume of passion.

I live within the cup of the crowned poets,
I am the chant of the Bacchantes.
I am the love of the starry heavens,
I am the song of songs...

The honey of thy lips agitates my inner most parts,
thus, I feel that I love Thee...
Thou art the mountain of myrrh,
and the hill of frankincense...
Thou art the fire of the Arcanum...
Thou art the erotic alp,
and the delectable smile
where love has become undressed...

Now, happy with the immortal wine,
let us ignite a bonfire and let us chant the Valkiries
with a triumphant chant
of flames and poetry.

Let the liquor come, let the light and music come...
Let the couples dance upon the soft carpet.
Let the Rose of Sharon sparkle within the cups,
and let the fire devour the shadows...

Let joy, fancy and poetry come...
Let us dance happily in the arms of love.
Never mind the sayings.
Let us enjoy together in the nuptial chamber,
within spikenards and myrrhs,
and let us chant our triumphal hymn
of light and poetry...

CHAPTER 17
Beelzebub and His Revolution

Everything in life is a matter of customs. A fornicator is an individual who has intensely accustomed his genital organs to copulate. Yet, if the same individual changes his custom of copulation to the custom of no copulation, then he transforms himself into a chaste person.

We have as an example the astonishing case of Mary Magdalene, who was a famous prostitute. Mary Magdalene became the famous Saint Mary Magdalene, the repented prostitute. Mary Magdalene became the chaste disciple of Christ.

Paul of Tarsus, the furious persecutor of Gnostics, received the sacred Initiation after the event which occurred to him on his way to Damascus. He left the custom of persecuting the Christians, and he adopted the Gnostic customs. So, he became a Gnostic Christian prophet.

An evil one can become a saint, if he changes his customs of evil for the customs of a saint.

After this preamble, let us enter into the interesting theme of our present chapter.

In our present Terrestrial Period, Beelzebub, the ancient prince of demons, reached a degree of perversity that is impossible to describe with words.

When any Magician wished to call Beelzebub in the Astral plane, he had to arm himself with very terrific courage in order to confront the most monstrous beast that the innumerable cycles of historic evolution have known.

The Magician would pronounce the sinister mantras of tenebrous evocations, which are written as follows:

"Antia rara ra ra........" which are pronounced like this:

"Aaaaaannnn.........

"tiiiiiiiiiii.............?

"aaaaaaaa!

"raaa.............

"*ra*...........?

"*ra*...........?

"*ra*...........!*"*

Then, the name of Beelzebub was called three times.

A breeze of death cooled the atmosphere of the evocator, and the prince of demons would answer with a terrifying roar, which seemed to emerge from all of the caverns of the earth.

Beelzebub answered the call of such a courageous Magician. Beelzebub's steps were like the trot of an infernal colt, and his presence was a thousand times more terrible, a thousand times more horrible, than death itself.

Woe unto the bold one who dared to call the prince of demons without being properly prepared! Woe unto such an intrepid one because he died under the claws of the horrible beast!

Yet, the very well disciplined Magician, firm as a warrior, extended his right hand towards the prince of demons and conjured him with the following words:

"*In the name of Jupiter, father of all gods, I conjure you, Te Vigos Cossilim!*" Then, the monster remained still.

His presence was like a gigantic, long haired gorilla. He embraced his disciples or friends with his long tail while talking with them.

His eyes were like a bull, his nose like a horse, his mouth like a mule, his feet and hands were enormous and horrible, and his body, as we have said, was hairy like the body of a gorilla.

He wore upon his head a biretta; upon his shoulders was the black cape of the prince of demons and a cord with seven knots was around his waist. All of these garments indicated that he was a prince of demons, a black magician of the 13th black initiation.

When he signed a pact with the black magicians, he signed the following upon the document: "Bel tengo mental la petra, y que a el la anduve sedra vao genizar ledes."

Beelzebub knew how to momentarily abandon the Astral plane in order to enter into the physical plane. This is how he became visible and tangible for his daring evocators in the physical plane.

He was making those who were signing pacts with him rich. Consequently, the souls of the evocators remained slaves of Beelzebub. He was giving them money, yet the evocators had to resolve to follow Beelzebub in a determined moment, in a determined day, hour, and minute.

This was because Beelzebub demanded the evocator's own life and the soul of his most beloved son. Beelzebub himself disincarnated the evocator in order to take him and place him under his service.

I know of a rich landholder who has signed a pact with another demon who is not Beelzebub. Every year a laborer mysteriously disappears from his farm.

One little girl watched her mother precisely in the very moment in which she disappeared, snatched by the mysterious hand of someone who was not seen. Consequently, this child remained an orphan. The black magicians can take their victims into the Astral plane, even with their bodies of flesh and bones, in order to place them under their service within that plane.

Many will say that the former statement is impossible, that the author of this book is getting more pesky than a fly. Yet, I recommend to those people to study *The Initiatic Novel of Occultism* by Krumm-Heller (Huiracocha), so they can learn about the history of the Holy Grail.

The Holy Grail was in the physical plane, yet now it is within the Astral plane. Also in the Astral plane is the temple of the Holy Grail, which was physical in the past, and also part of the mountain of Monserrate in Cataluña (Spain). This is what is called the Jinn State.

This chalice is filled with the blood of the Redeemer of the world, which Joseph of Arimathea collected when he was at the foot of the cross in Golgotha.

We read in Krumm Heller's book how Commander Montero entered with his physical body into the authentic Rosicrucian Temple of Chapultepec (Mexico). This temple is in a Jinn State, so Commander Montero entered into this temple with his body in a Jinn state.

Dr. Rudolf Steiner, the great German doctor, said: "A physical body can enter into the internal worlds without losing its physical characteristics."

Mario Roso de Luna made beautiful studies about the Jinn lands. Don Mario Roso de Luna died disappointed with the Theosophical society.

The Rosicross is one of seven Initiatic sanctuaries which are located in the Astral plane. Yet, all of the Rosicrucian schools which are presently known in this physical world are false ever since such schools fell into the hands of Javhe.

The natives of America knew about the Jinn states in depth. Therefore, when the Spanish conquistadors arrived, they hid their most sacred temples within the Astral plane. As a result, the Mayan mysteries were saved from the Spaniard's profanation. The Sanctuary of Mayan Mysteries is one of the seven great occult sanctuaries which now remain within the Astral plane.

When a physical body is active within the Astral plane, it remains subjected to the laws of that plane without losing its physiological characteristics.

I know about a fellow who robbed two gold bars from the profound cave of the Pregoneros (State of Merida, Venezuela). When the man in question went out of this cave, he felt that these two gold bars were moving in his hands and simultaneously a storm was unleashed. He then saw that his two gold bars had transformed into two horrible snakes. This man then threw them out of his hands and flew away in terror.

What also can occur is that a disincarnated person can momentarily abandon the Astral plane and penetrate into the physical plane. Such an individual becomes invisible for those persons from the Astral plane; yet, he remains tangible for the people of this physical world. In such a case, the disincarnated person remains momentarily subjected to the laws which command the physical plane without his Astral Body losing its own characteristics.

These cases are counted in thousands within the apparition archives of psychic societies. These are the apparitions of deceased persons about which the spiritists speak. Nonetheless, they never know how to explain them. Superficially, they say that these are materialization phenomena, and they fill them with millions of theories.

They ignore that the soul can enter into the distinct departments of the kingdom. What is necessary is to know how to do it, as the Magicians do.

Therefore, the Magician does not need spiritist mediums in order to perform these phenomena of practical magic.

When magic is explained as it really is, it seems to make no sense to fanatical people. They prefer to follow their world of illusions.

I know the case of an evocator who called Beelzebub with the Clavicle (clue) of Solomon, which is as follows:

> *Agion tetra-gram vaicheon estimilia maton espares retragramaton orgoran irion.*
>
> *Erglion existion eryona omera brasin moim mesias soler, emmanuel Sabaoth Adonai. I praise thee and I invoke thee.*

When the evocator saw Beelzebub in the middle of the room, he became filled with infinite terror and did not dare make any pact with him for he became tongue-tied.

Beelzebub always had his cavern filled with weapons and seals in order to mark the Astral bodies of his disciples.

I, Samael Aun Weor, was always observing Beelzebub in the Astral plane. I tried to gain his affection because what kept calling my attention was the overwhelming fact that he was irradiating love towards his friends.

He was a very rare and unique case among his kind because I had never heard of a demon whose aura irradiated a blue light, which is that of love.

Certainly, he was always hurling terrible threats upon me. Yet, I always defeated him with my mantras, and thus I accompanied him into his caverns within the Astral plane. I reached even to the point of taking part in his feasts, pretending to be a black magician, and even his comrade. This was in order to more closely study this personage.

My intentions in the long run were to perform the greatest task in the cosmos, which was to take Beelzebub out from the Black Lodge and transform him into a disciple of the White Lodge.

My disciples considered this task to be something truly impossible. Beelzebub did not stop threatening me; nevertheless, in spite of everything, I did not dismay.

Finally, there was a curious event which assured my intentions. One night, I, along with a chela, invoked Beelzebub in the Astral plane. Once he answered our call, we invited him to dinner. He accepted our invitation, and we went into a restaurant of the Astral plane. As we already explained, the Astral Body also eats elements which are related to its organism. Thus, the Astral world is almost similar to our own physical world.

So, I asked for food for Beelzebub, while I contented myself to drink a glass of water. When Beelzebub sat at the table, he took the biretta off from his head and began to eat in a gentleman-like manner.

It was intriguing to see that type of gorilla eating at the table like a great lord. Some chelas who were in that place addressed me and told me that I was being disrespectful in bringing a demon into that place.

As was expected, they were looking at him with disgust, and soon they began to vacate the place. Notwithstanding, I answered them, "This is also a man and he deserves to be respected."

Then, Beelzebub took the floor and, in a profoundly sad tone, said, "Everybody despises me; the only one who does not despise me is my friend Samael Aun Weor."

This was the Astral experience that encouraged me to continue with my longed for purpose, which was to take Beelzebub out from the Black Lodge and to make him a disciple of the White Fraternity.

Some people would see the fact that the Astral Body can eat and drink as something impossible, because their unsound mysticism is always telling them that the Astral Body is something vague, a vaporous fluid, an intangible and non-material body. Considering they are only theorists, it does not occur to them to verify it.

Let such ladies and gentlemen study Vivekananda's books in order for them to be informed that the internal bodies (Astral Body, etc.) are also material.

This is why we, the Gnostics, say that nothing can exist, not even God, without the help of matter.

So, the Astral Body is material, and it is a dense organism like the physical body. The fact that matter, in its last synthesis, is reduced to energy, does not deny its existence once in that state. If we cannot see it with our sense of sight, it is because it belongs to the fifth dimension. Our physical eyes will not serve for seeing the Astral plane until we make them suitable for this purpose or until we place ourselves into the Astral plane with our physical body. Thus, the Astral organism is as dense as the physical organism, yet it belongs to another department of the kingdom.

The Astral Body is much more sensitive than the physical body. The Astral organism is like a duplicate of the physical organism. As the physical body has to be nourished with food related to its nature, so does the Astral Body.

The occultist utilizes the Astral Body for his studies and for his great investigations, because such a body is advantageously arranged over the physical body. Time and distance do not exist for the Astral Body, and what one learns through it remains immediately recorded within the consciousness of the Being forever.

Therefore, my dear reader, do not take the fact that I was having dinner with Beelzebub in the Astral plane as something strange.

Many times I had asked for the attention of Beelzebub's Innermost, in order for Him to do something for His soul, but the answer of his Innermost (Spirit) was, "I cannot, he does not obey me. I have fought a lot; yet, it is impossible." Beelzebub, as all black magicians from the school of Sodom, considered that the Spirit is inferior and the soul is superior. This is because they say that the soul is more psychic.

So, Beelzebub, as well as the disciples from the school of Sodom, were convinced that the Guardian of the Threshold was their Real Being. Precisely, this is why Beelzebub did not listen to his Innermost.

Beelzebub ignored that he was in evil. He furiously attacked the White Magicians and believed them to be perverse. He was feeling himself to be a saint and good and considered the White Magicians to be demons.

He ignored our Gnostic principle which states, "One has a soul, and one is a Spirit."

The Testament of Learning says:

> Before the false dawn came over this earth, those who survived the hurricane and the storm gave praise to the Innermost, and to them appeared the heralds of the dawn.

The Intimate or Innermost is our internal sun. Thus, the soul who removes itself from its Innermost falls into the abyss.

The Spirit is our Real Being. The soul who removes itself from its own Spirit is disintegrated. This is the Second Death.

As a result of the words that Beelzebub uttered in the middle of that dinner, I, filled with enthusiasm, performed another experiment. I invoked him anew within the Astral plane. Once Beelzebub attended my call, I politely invited him to have some drinks with me. Beelzebub happily and joyfully accepted my invitation.

While Beelzebub and I were walking in the Astral plane, I was changing Beelzebub's own vibration. Finally, I succeeded and I removed him out of the Astral plane and took him into the most divine plane of consciousness of the cosmos.

This most divine plane of the cosmos is named "The Pass Not Ring" in the first volume of *The Secret Doctrine* by the Master Blavatsky.

If we consider the cosmos as a great tree with its roots in the Absolute, then these roots will be the "Pass Not Ring" because no one can pass that plane, not even the greatest Gods of the cosmos can pass beyond that ring.

Beelzebub was really overwhelmed before the tremendous luminosity of that ineffable region. Its beauty and happiness are indescribable. Yet, he felt terror because for four eternities Beelzebub had lived within the darkness of the tenebrous caverns.

When seeing the light he felt fear, and so with a hoarse voice he uttered, "This is unceasingly terrifying."

I responded, "More terrifying is the darkness in which you live." Then, walking through this plane, we passed in front of a house.

"Can I enter?" he asked me, and I answered him affirmatively. Immediately we entered and stayed inside for a while.

Really, everything was new for Beelzebub. He was feeling discontent because he was accustomed to living among the veiled prophets, and the tremendous luminosity of that plane was horrifyingly bothering him.

After this interval of light, I took him again to the other extreme, into the terrible darkness of the Avitchi (Hell) of our earth, where one does not see anything but pieces of souls in the state of disintegration. There you find souls of prostitutes who by means of too much copulation became totally separated from their Innermost. Now, while lying down upon their filthy beds, they are disintegrating themselves like candles, melting with the fire of their passion.

We found there souls of demons who were nothing else but pieces. "Here I feel a little bit better," said Beelzebub to me.

I answered him, "You have to accustom yourself to the light."

He then stated, "It is very hard to do so because I have been living within the darkness for a very long time."

When showing him the pieces of souls, I warned him, "Here is where you will end up if you continue with your evilness." Then after, I took him again into his Astral plane.

Despite the fact that I was not content with the former ordeal, I did not dismay. I understood that he had the Guardian of the Threshold within his internal bodies. As a logical fact, in spite of the promising hopes that I was observing in Beelzebub, that Guardian (which is so respected by the black magicians) was totally enslaving him. Nevertheless, Beelzebub did not get furious against the light, the light only annoyed him.

He was suffering greatly in the Astral plane because all the spiritualists were turning up their noses at him and he was very discouraged by these people.

There was always the same despot behind the altar commanding his temple. He was always around the same vices, and those vices had already made of him a gorilla, a filthy beast.

I, Samael Aun Weor, understood all of this. Therefore, I did not dismay, especially when he was trying to feel affection for me and was considering me his best friend.

Thus, I performed a third experiment. This one was really the decisive one. I took Beelzebub into the "Pass Not Ring" for a second time. While there, I invoked for him his best and very ancient friends from the epoch of Saturn.

These friends of his are now in this present time luminous Lords of the mind, Lords of the light. Filled with pain, they hugged Beelzebub. One of them said to him, "I never imagined reaching the point of seeing you in this state."

Then, Beelzebub answered, "You see how far I went."

In that plane, Beelzebub seemed to be something like a gorilla from the African jungle within an elegant hall of Paris.

Nevertheless, when Beelzebub recognized his most beloved friends, he was appalled within the depths of his soul and totally comprehended how he had gone astray.

This was Beelzebub, the simpatico and handsome man of Arcadia. If it were not for the taverns, he would not have known the horrifying black magician who misguided him.

Then, I asked permission of the Masters of that luminous plane to leave Beelzebub in that luminous region for some time. The Masters joyfully agreed with my petition with the condition that I constantly visit him.

We then together made a chain of love around Beelzebub, inundating him with our love and filling him with our best atoms, saturating him with light and splendor.

I constantly visited Beelzebub. He was always sad, since he was the only gorilla within that plane of Gods. All of the Beings of that region looked at him with curiosity, and his ancient friends of the Saturnine period were advising and helping him.

So, Beelzebub was accustoming himself little by little to the light, and he was feeling remorse in the bottom of his soul for the lost time. He felt shame when in front of his best friends and he longed for personal improvement.

Therefore, we helped him by temporarily uniting him with his Internal God, with his own Innermost, and a supreme effort was made by his "Glorian" in order to call his soul to the union with his Innermost.

When reaching this part of our book, it will be rare for the occultists to have heard about the Glorian. In reality, the Glorian is none other than the Ray from which the Innermost (Spirit) emanated. Thus, the Glorian is substance, yet it is not Spirit, nor is it matter.

The Glorian is the Great Breath that is profoundly unknowable to itself. It is a breath from the Absolute, one of the many breaths of the Great Breath.

The Glorian is the "Atmic Thread" of the Hindus. It is the Absolute within us, our own individual Ray, the whole of our real Being made in glory.

The soul aspires for union with his Innermost, and the Innermost aspires for union with his Glorian.

The diocese of our Glorian is the turk chair of our organism. This turk chair is formed by the cervical vertebrae of our spinal column. Here is where the Glorian has its silver atoms. When Beelzebub became united with his Glorian, the white light of the Glorian was shining with all of its splendor in that part of Beelzebub's Astral organism.

This momentary fusion of Beelzebub with his Innermost took away from him that horrifying appearance of a gorilla. Dressed with the vestures of his Innermost, he assumed the shape of that simpatico young man of Arcadia.

We must not forget that the atoms of the Glorian are of silver, and that the Holy Grail is of silver and not of gold as some Rosicrucians suppose. Hence, the Chalice which the Initiates of the God Sirius carry over the hood of their forehead is of silver. Any chela who visits the Transcended Church of the Star Sirius will convince himself of my affirmation.

A great interior revolution was taking place within Beelzebub. So, one night, a most quiet and silent night, I made some experiments of Theurgy which were really definitive.

I projected for Beelzebub upon the cosmic scenario some scenes of the Akashic records. The primeval epochs from the Saturnine period were appearing, epochs in which Beelzebub still was a good and simple man, when he still did not have vices, when he still was not a friend of brothels or taverns.

All of those scenes were moving themselves in a successive order. Beelzebub was silently contemplating them. Then after, the taverns, the little parties, the social nights, and the brothels with their orgies appeared.

Beelzebub, filled with a terrible internal emotion, was contemplating those very ancient scenes and he was remembering his errors.

He was before the primeval causes which had conduced him towards his present state. A true revolution of Beelzebub was in activity. Beelzebub was revolutionizing against hatred, against selfishness, against vices, against fornication, against anger, against crime, etc.

Suddenly, something dreadful and horrifying emerged from within that scene. It was a being who was an abominable demon, dressed in a black tunic, and who was wearing in his ears two rings. The eyes of such a demon were protruding outwardly and an atmosphere of profound darkness enveloped him.

Beelzebub remained astonished when contemplating him, since he was his very ancient Master. He was that horrifying black magician who, with his marvelous clues, was always making Beelzebub triumphant in the vice of gambling. He was that horrifying demon who had led him towards the first black initiation.

This demon was the one who had enslaved Beelzebub to the Guardian of the Threshold in that very ancient tenebrous temple where Beelzebub passed the first ritual. It is the same ritual through which, in this day and age, the black magicians pass.

This sinister personage approached Beelzebub, smiling in order to greet him. Beelzebub, as when one is attracted by a hypnotic spell, wanted to approach him in order to return the greetings. Yet, he stopped, and a gesture of rebellion emerged from within the bottom of his soul. Heroically he exclaimed, "No I do not greet you; I do not want anything from you, since you are responsible for me being in this state!"

Then, the sinister personage, with a very hoarse voice, which seemed to emerge from within the bottom of the centuries and from within the tenebrous caverns, answered, "Is this the payment which you give for my services? Have you already forgotten my sacrifices? Have you already forgotten the teachings that I gave you? You are allowing yourself to be guided on the bad path."

Yet Beelzebub, filled with energy, answered, "I do not want to listen to you, since you are responsible for me being in this state. So, I believe I have paid you for the granted favors."

Then, I conjured this sinister personage in order for him to withdraw. Hence, the black magician withdrew with his profound darkness. He seemed to sink himself into the abyss.

This was an ordeal for Beelzebub, and he emerged successful in this ordeal. Beelzebub revolutionized himself against black magic. A gesture of rebellion was bursting forth from within the bottom of his soul.

After having projected these Akashic Records in the atmosphere for the sake of Beelzebub, we, the Masters and my disciples, performed chains of love together in order to irradiate light to Beelzebub.

Afterwards, I projected in the form of pictures the fate which was awaiting for him if he would still follow the black path. Pictures appeared of Beelzebub happy in the taverns and delivering himself to all the vices of the earth. Finally, the setting of the Cosmic Night was appearing, and all the seas overflowed over the earth. Everything was in ruins and ice. There, thrown away on a shore was a piece of the head and the chest and arms of the one who had been Beelzebub in the past.

Once the former picture concluded, I then told him, "Lo and behold the doom which is awaiting for you if you keep following the black path."

Afterwards, I projected the pictures of the fate which was awaiting for him if he would follow the path of White Magic. In these pictures Beelzebub was shown already united with his Innermost, dressed in the tunic of Mastery with its long cape of a Hierophant and with his scepter of power. A luminous garden appeared, and Beelzebub was treading upon this garden as an omnipotent and heavenly God.

I told him, "This is the providence which awaits for you if you follow the path of White Magic. Thus, resolve yourself now! Do you follow White Magic or do you continue on the black path?"

Beelzebub's firm answer was, "I stay with White Magic." Then, Beelzebub fell down on his knees weeping as when a child weeps. Raising his eyes towards heaven, he closed his hands together over his chest, and among tears and sobs, he prayed to heaven.

He was a repented demon. His horns were shining upon his forehead as if they already wanted to vanish with the light.

The Major Brethren hugged him with tears in their eyes. All of them rejoiced amongst themselves while a triumphal and delectable march with its ineffable melodies played in the starry heavens of Urania.

I say unto you, that likewise joy shall be in heaven over one sinner that repenteth, more than over ninety and nine just persons, which need no repentance. LUKE 15:7

Then, I kneeled and prostrated myself before the most powerful Hierarch of the cosmos, who is called by the Tibetans "the Mother of Mercy" or "the Melodious Voice Oeaoeh." He is the Only Begotten, the great universal Word of life, whose body is all of the sounds which are played in the Infinite. His beauty is ineffable. He bears a crown with three points, and his very long cape is carried by the Elohim. They carry the long train of his cape.

So, I begged the Only Begotten to have Beelzebub close to Him, in order for Him to adjust Beelzebub's Kundalini.

Beelzebub's Kundalini was flowing downwards, forming the tail (Kundabuffer) of the demon. Now, the Only Begotten's duty was to raise Beelzebub's Kundalini upwards, towards his head, in order to convert him into an Angel.

The Master (the Only Begotten) accepted my supplication and, within that plane of diamantine light, he placed Beelzebub within a resplendent garden and gave him a cosmic book for him to study. He instructed him in the path of light and filled him with atoms of wisdom.

Later on, I made Beelzebub "revive" the whole of his life throughout all of the four great cosmic periods, and I showed him the beautiful fate which was awaiting for him if he was going to follow the luminous path.

When Beelzebub saw himself already converted into a Hierarch of the future, he asked me, "Would this be soon?" I answered him affirmatively.

Afterwards, when he finished reviving all of these scenes, he then arrived before the only Son (only Begotten), saying, "I come with my soul transformed." The Master then continued helping him, and his Kundalini arose. Thus, the tail (Kundabuffer) of the demon disappeared from him.

Nonetheless, the horns were still over his forehead, because these horns belong to the Guardian of the Threshold, and he was closely fused with the Guardian of the Threshold. This internal beast was a terrible obstacle for his evolution. It was necessary to cast this beast out from him in order to liberate him from this internal monster which held him in bondage for innumerable ages.

That internal monster had taken possession of his will, of his thought, of his consciousness, of everything. Therefore, the necessity of expelling him out from his own Being, in order to perform a fast internal progress, was peremptory.

This then was the moment when I took him into the Astral plane in order to submit him to the first Initiatic ordeal, through which anyone who wants to reach the Initiation has to irremediably pass. This is the ordeal of the Guardian of the Threshold.

In this ordeal, when we invoke this monster, he comes out from within ourselves and he threateningly thrusts himself against us.

Beelzebub had to invoke his own Guardian many times. Finally, a horrifying breeze blew everywhere and then, in a dreadful and threatening way, the spectre of the Threshold appeared. That creature was a giant, about three meters in stature, and his body had two meters of thickness. He had the appearance of a monstrous gorilla with a flat, round face, two horns, and protruding eyes.

Beelzebub had fortified this monster throughout the ages. Now, Beelzebub did not have any other choice but to fight him. Therefore, Beelzebub courageously thrust himself towards the monster and subsequently defeated him.

This was the monster that gave Beelzebub that horrifying appearance of a gorilla. This was the beast of the Threshold. Hence, a "dry" noise resounded within space, which is different than the metallic sound produced in similar cases with our present disciples. This is because Beelzebub is from another World Period.

Afterwards, Beelzebub was welcomed within the Children's Hall with great festivity and delectable music, and so, he remained converted into a disciple of the Major Brethren.

The Masters gave him a symbolic cup of silver.

After Beelzebub passed through this first ordeal, I then took him again to the Only Begotten in order for the Only Begotten to keep helping him.

The horns disappeared from the forehead of Beelzebub, because these horns belonged to his internal beast, to the Guardian of the Threshold, which is called by the Rosicrucians from the school of Sodom "The Guardian of their Chamber," and also "The Guardian of their Sanctum."

The monstrous figure of the gorilla also disappeared from Beelzebub, because that figure was not his own, but the figure of the Guardian of the Threshold, which is called by the Rosicrucians from the school of Sodom "The Guardian of their Consciousness."

Beelzebub beautified himself. Nevertheless, he now had to accomplish that saying of the Master:

> Render therefore unto Caesar the things which are Caesar's; and unto God the things that are God's." MATTHEW 22:21

Beelzebub had to return to the black magicians all the articles which he had from them: the biretta, the seven knotted cord, and the cape of the prince of demons. Also, he had to erase his name from the book where it was written.

When reaching this part of our present chapter, we have to give some explanations about this matter, because many readers would think it strange that we talk about books within the Astral world. It is because people are accustomed to think that the Astral world is a vague, fluid, vaporous, intangible, immaterial, etc. world.

We, the Gnostics, are essentially realistic and we have reached the conclusion that nothing can exist, not even God, without the help of matter, even though what is matter is something absolutely unknown to the so-called materialistic schools.

Such schools are nothing else but a theoretical "cage of parrots," because in reality these know-it-alls of materialism truly do not know anything else but the grossest states of matter. For example, what do they know about occult chemistry, the anatomy, and the ultra-biology of the internal bodies of the human being?

Materialistic skepticism is the result of a cerebral dementia. This has already been confirmed by the psychiatric doctors of Paris when they analyzed the brain of an existentialist.

In reality, within each normal human being, there exists a true, natural mystic who is without any type of aberration. This is because the materialistic, as well as the spiritualistic theories, are equally filled with aberrations and fantasies. Therefore, we, the Gnostics, are not spiritualists, neither materialists, but we are realists.

We deeply know about the infinite manifestations of matter and the Spirit, and we know that the fundamental base of the Being is neither Spirit nor matter. The Glorian is a substance which gives its substance to itself, yet it is neither Spirit nor matter.

Therefore, when we affirm that Beelzebub had to erase his name from the book of a temple, we speak with as much authority as when we say that we have to erase a name from a physical-material book. If material objects exist in this physical plane, likewise material solid objects exist within the Astral region, because the Astral plane is as material as the physical plane. Moreover, we can visit the Astral plane any time we want by penetrating within it with our physical body of flesh and bones, dressed and prepared as if we are going on the street for a walk.

Books of Astral matter exist within every temple of black magic. The names of its affiliates are written in these books. Whenever a black magician withdraws from a temple of black magic, he must always erase his name from the book where it is written. Also, he has to return all of the articles to their owners:

> Render therefore unto Caesar the things which are Caesar's; and unto God the things that are God's. MATTHEW 22:21

So, after the ordeal of the Guardian of the Threshold, Beelzebub presented himself to his tenebrous temple in order to erase his name from the book where it was written.

It was an enormous, gigantic temple of black magic. The Great Hierarch of the temple was behind the altar. When he saw Beelzebub, impatiently and irritably he exclaimed, "You finally remember to come? Since you are the one who directs this temple, why do you delay so much in coming?"

Then, Beelzebub answered with an energetic tone, "I do not belong to this temple anymore. I am now following the path of White Magic." Afterwards, he took the biretta from his head and the cord from his waist and thrust them over the altar while saying, "There, I leave these things to you. I do not need them anymore, since now I am of the White Lodge." Then he added, "Give me the book so I can erase my name from it."

Then, the tenebrous priest answered in a despotic way, "Look for the book yourself; I will not give myself that duty."

Thus, Beelzebub looked for the book, and then after, he erased his name and departed from the temple with a firm and triumphant step.

Subsequently, we directed ourselves to a certain tenebrous cavern, where he had to deliver the cape of the Prince of Demons.

When Beelzebub entered into the black cavern, he spoke the following, "I come to deliver this cape that does not belong to me anymore, because I am now a disciple of the White Lodge." And so he thrust the cape towards them. Beelzebub departed from that cavern, while the black magicians from that cavern insulted him.

Once out of that cavern, we directed ourselves to Beelzebub's own cavern. Here, innumerable weapons and seals of black magic were shown. Beelzebub burnt all of these with the salamanders of fire.

This is how, my beloved reader, the former prince of demons "Beelzebub" was liberated from black magic.

Beelzebub continued abiding within the light of the "Pass Not Ring" and the only Son (Begotten) kept teaching him.

Some days after, the ordeal of the Great Guardian of the Threshold of the World was presented to him. This is the second ordeal which every disciple must pass through. Beelzebub courageously confronted the second Guardian. Another party was celebrated in another temple, and another symbolic cup of silver was delivered to him.

When the second ordeal is passed, then another ordeal comes in order to burn with fire the residue which remains within the disciple.

Beelzebub entered within the hall of fire and he courageously sustained himself within the flames. This is the third ordeal, and Beelzebub passed it very well. The fire burnt all of the larvae of his Astral Body; thus, he remained clean.

Later on, he passed through the four ordeals and proved that he was capable, even capable to kiss the whip of the executioner. These ordeals are the ordeals of Earth, Fire, Water, and Air.

Beelzebub courageously passed through these four ordeals. Then, he received the cape of chela (disciple) of the White Lodge, and he dressed himself with a purple tunic.

Beelzebub became a disciple of the White Lodge and he totally sanctified himself.

For such a motive, the Great Brethren celebrated with a grand cosmic party. The Divine Rabbi of Galilee received him with open arms, and the Divine Rabbi congratulated me, Samael Aun Weor, because of my triumph.

This event remained written in the book of the twenty and four Elders, and the cosmos, the whole of it, was shaken.

This is the greatest event of cosmic evolution because I have heard about fallen angels, yet I have never heard of a repented demon.

So, Beelzebub delivered himself to healing sick people and to taking them by night in their Astral bodies into the Temple of Alden for their healing. He delivered himself to goodness, to righteousness, and to justice. He changed his demonic customs for the customs of a saint, and hence he became a saint.

Therefore, the main link, which was Beelzebub, was lost, and panic sprouted within the Black Lodge.

The black magicians unfolded ancient parchments and were astonished when reading the innumerable degrees which Beelzebub had and how now, "in a manner of speaking," he had betrayed them. Some of them were commenting on this case by saying, "Now we have nobody but our chief Javhe, the 'Boss.' If he abandons us, then we are lost."

Afterwards, when Beelzebub passed through the four ordeals of Earth, Fire, Water, and Air, he visited Javhe, his former chief, and he said to him, "I come to say farewell to you, because now I am no longer dependent on your government, for now I am a disciple of the White Lodge."

Javhe then furiously answered, "Traitor! Miserable one! Renegade! You allowed yourself to be convinced by Samael Aun Weor. Yet, he does not have your degrees, neither mine as well. Be aware that you are walking on the bad path."

Then, Beelzebub answered him in an energetic tone, "The one who is walking on the bad path is you. I follow Samael Aun Weor. I did not see the light, but since Samael has shown it to me, I will not leave this light anymore, and I follow Samael Aun Weor in the same way that all of his disciples follow him."

Javhe then said to him, "Damned! Damned! Damned! My damnation will follow you eternally."

Yet, Beelzebub answered him with a smile, "Your damnation does not enter me because I am protected by the White Lodge."

After Beelzebub had spoken, Javhe then turned himself against me, saying, "You are the one to whom I have to attack, because you are responsible for all of this." Subsequently, he attacked me with all of his sinister occult power, yet I easily conjured him, and I defeated him.

Beelzebub kept healing the sick. However, the instant in which he had to ask for a physical body, in order to climb up on the path of the Initiation, approached with necessity.

So, Beelzebub asked for a physical body. His petition was accepted, and he inscribed himself in the ninth Karmic office. This is how he entered into our human evolution.

The Initiate Gargha Kuichin generously offered his cooperation in order for Beelzebub to take a physical body within his home, yet this was completely impossible, due to health reasons of his wife. She could not endure the tremendous vibration of Beelzebub.

However, the Major Brethren had foreseen everything very well. The "chela" Beelzebub incarnated himself in France, in a feminine body. Now Beelzebub is a beautiful girl in France, who will overwhelm the world because of her sanctity, power, and wisdom.

Her parents have a young and beautiful marriage in which only love and comprehension reigns, because both are Initiates. They are laborers, yet they enjoy a simple and beautiful life.

Beelzebub was born with the body of a girl because the feminine body is indispensable for the development of feelings, tenderness, and love. Now, Beelzebub, already with a physical body, can rapidly pass the Nine Initiations of Minor Mysteries, and finally, he will unite himself with his Innermost. Thus, he will convert himself into a Master of Major Mysteries from the White Fraternity.

From the great sinners, the ones great in virtue are born.

The Sapience of Sin

Wisdom is elaborated with the sapience of sin,
and the vertigo of the Absolute.
Oh defeated Magdala!
Thy withered lips due to too many kisses,
also know how to love....

Therefore, I love Thee,
fallen woman,
I die for Thee,
no matter what they say.

I like dancing and thy love.
Alas! Woman do not leave me,
for I die for Thee.
Alas! Woman do not leave me,
for I only love Thee.

The forbidden fruit makes us gods.
Thy delectable words of love,
and thy grave oaths,
are like the fire of the roses,
and like those delectable moments
which no one knows of...

The greatest angels
were always devils
from great Bacchanalias;
they enjoyed the lips of love,
they sung the song of songs...

Red roses are better than white,
because they have the sapience of sin
and the vertigo of the Absolute,
and because they have wept a lot,
a sweet Nazarene has forgiven them....

Temptation is the mother of sin,
and the pain of sin is the sapience.
Christ loved she who had wept much,
and said to her: "Woman, I forgive Thee,
for Thou hast loved much..."

The most divine Gods
are those who have been more human;
the most divine Gods
are those who were Devils.

Chant! Oh Beelzebub, chant thy song,
Chant! Oh Beelzebub, a chant of love.
Woman, thou art a rose of passion,
Thou hast a thousand delectable names,
yet, thy true name is love...
I want to fasten laurels to thy temples,
I want to kiss thy lips with love...

I want to tell Thee rare things,
I want to tell Thee intimate things,
I want to tell Thee everything,
within the perfumed room of mahogany.
I want to tell Thee everything in starry nights.
Thou art the star of Dawn,
Thou art the light of Aubade...

Thy breasts pour honey and venom,
and the liquor of the female
is a liquor of Mandrake.
It is a summit, an immensity, a fire.
It is the ardent and adored flame,
through which one enters into heaven...

And I saw the beast, and the kings of the earth, and their armies,
gathered together to make war against him that sat on the horse, and
against his army. - Revelation 19:19

CHAPTER 18
The Millenium

When the main link from the Black Lodge was broken, the revolution of Beelzebub extended itself over the whole face of the Earth. Concurrently, the Millennium began exactly in the year 1950.

The foundations of the world were being shaken and other black magicians followed the example of Beelzebub.

Astaroth, an inseparable friend of Beelzebub, and Santa Maria, the comrade of Mariela, the great black magician, also followed the example of Beelzebub.

Thus, the Revolution of Beelzebub is marching on. Everywhere the oppressed are rising against the oppressors and everywhere are wars and rumors of wars. What is already agonizingly old is holding onto life while what is new wants to be born and live.

The Revolution of Beelzebub is on the march. The age of Aquarius is reigning and the storm of exclusivity has been unleashed with all of its fury. Parties are struggling against other parties, religions against religions; nations thrust themselves to war and each hand is risen against other hands. Everything which is obsolete, everything which is old, fights to survive while the new wants to impose itself.

It is the struggle of two epochs: one which is dying and the other which is being born. We have entered into the Millennium. This human evolution has failed. Almost all of the human beings who presently live upon the face of the Earth have already received the mark of the beast upon their foreheads. They are demons.

The billions of souls who are presently incarnated are demon souls, perverse souls. Only a handful of souls were saved.

The Astral plane was filled with trillions of demons who were fighting terribly in order to win the great war in order to establish their worldly government. This plan is inscribed within the *Protocols of Zion*.

Javhe and his Black Lodge were already at the point of total triumph upon the Earth; everything was marching in accordance with their plans.

The tempest was at its peak. The age of Aquarius was approaching and there was not even a ray of hope within the darkness of hatred.

The Second World War had just passed and millions of disincarnated souls within the different theaters of war were still in our Astral environment, thirsty for blood.

This is when the Venerable White Lodge delivered into my hands *"the key of the bottomless pit and a great chain"* in order for the first verse of the twentieth chapter of the Apocalypse (Revelation) to be accomplished, which states:

> *And I saw an angel come down from heaven, having the key of the bottomless pit and a great chain in his hand.*
> REVELATION 20:1

I received commands from the Lords of Karma in order to lock Javhe and all of the black magicians within the abyss.

This task was certainly overwhelming for me, yet I felt omnipotent, because after submitting me to the tremendous ordeals of the Initiation, the Venerable Masters delivered to me the sword of justice and a white horse. Thus, the greatest honor granted to a human being, which is to "judge" and to initiate the age of Aquarius, was given to me.

A band was placed on my thigh which states in symbolic letters: *"King of Kings, and Lord of Lords."* This was done in order to fulfill the sixteenth verse from the nineteenth chapter, which states:

> *And he hath on his vesture and on his thigh a name written, **King of Kings, and Lord of Lords**.*   REVELATION 19:16

I carry this band on my thigh in order to represent that the power of the human being is within the sex. Consequently, this is why the mission of teaching the tremendous secrets of sex for the first time to humanity was granted to me.

This is why the Innermost, the Intimate, or the Real Being of the one who writes this book, carries that band on his thigh. This is the way in which my particular mission is symbolized.

When the night in which I had to obey the command of seizing Javhe arrived, I marched with all of my disciples in a rigorous military formation. We began hailing Javhe, which is how we surrounded him and seized him by surprise. He was convinced that we were going to entertain him, therefore he did not escape from our hands.

Afterwards, we locked him within the Avitchi of the black moon. Seven atomic doors of iron usher one towards that plane of consciousness. The sword with which Michael defeated Luzbel and all of the tenebrous legions of ancient cosmic periods remains hanging on the great external door. The black magicians become horrified when they see that sword.

Javhe has a very grave Karma, since he was the secret perpetrator of the crucifixion of Christ, and he is also directly responsible for the failure of human evolution on the Earth. He has to irremediably pay these old debts, because no one can mock the law with impunity.

The Lords of Karma delivered to me a heavy cross covered with spikes in order to crucify Javhe upon it with his head downwards and his feet upwards. Since he crucified the Christ, now Karma has entered into action.

This was in order to fulfill the second and third verses from the twentieth chapter of the Apocalypse (Revelation) which state:

> And he laid hold on the dragon, that old serpent (Javhe), which is the Devil, and Satan, and bound him a thousand years.
>
> And cast him into the bottomless pit, and shut him up, and set a seal upon him, that he should deceive the nations no more, till the thousand years should be fulfilled: and after that he must be loosed a little season. REVELATION 20:2, 3

"A thousand years" signifies various thousands of years. In other words, Javhe and his people will remain within the abyss during the whole luminous cycle of Aquarius. Yet, in the cycle of Capricorn, the last opportunity for their repentance on our Earth will be granted to them.

The words "Dragon," "Demon" and "Satan" are individual and generic words, because these words symbolize Javhe and the billions of demon souls which I, Samael Aun Weor, am locking into the abyss.

When locating all the evil of the world, I was aware that the evil within Asia had its principal focus in China. All of the evil in the western world had its principal focus in Rome. I remembered that when one wants to kill a snake, one must aim for the snake's head; thus, I started capturing and taking into the abyss all of the black Hierarchs from other cosmic periods along with their trillions of demons.

I saw Luzbel with his red tunic and red turban. He was carrying a very ancient parchment rolled up in his tail.

I saw Ariman, the creator of gross materialism. Ariman wears a red tunic and red cap.

I saw Lusifuge Rofocale, creator of money.

I saw Orhuarpa, the founder of the mysteries of the tenebrous sun in Atlantis.

I saw Bael, the contrary pole of the luminous angel Adonai. The King Bael wears a crown. He taught his disciples from a great book within a cavern from the desert.

I saw the soldiers of Javhe, who assassinated the Christ. I disguised myself as an elder black magician in order to convince Luzbel that his boss Javhe was calling him with all of his legions.

Thus, I danced before them, and little by little, I led them into the abyss.

This is how Lucifer and his legions, Ariman and his legions, Lucifuge and his legions, Orhuarpa and his legions, Bael and his legions, Baal Pegor and his legions, were all brought down.

I performed marvels before these chiefs of legions: I danced, sung, played kettle drums, etc. To that end, I performed everything which was at my reach in order to clean the atmosphere of the world. I utilized all of my very ancient knowledge in order to lock up all of those billions of demons who already had the world within their claws.

I disguised myself in thousands of ways in order to take these black magicians into the abyss.

All of these black magicians with their people presented me with great combats within the Astral Light, yet I defeated them while mounted on a white horse and with the sword of justice in my mouth.

This is how verses 15 and 19 from the nineteenth chapter of the Apocalypse were accomplished, which state:

> *And out of his mouth goeth a sharp sword, that with it he should smite the nations: and he shall rule them with a rod of iron: and he treadeth the winepress of the fierceness and wrath of Almighty God.* REVELATION 19:15

> *And I saw the beast, and the kings of the earth, and their armies, gathered together to make war against him that sat on the horse, and against his army.* REVELATION 19:19

The Real Being or Innermost of the one who writes this book performed all of these marvels and He performed them well.

The one who writes this book is only the humble and rough personality of the Master Samael Aun Weor. This Master is my Real Being, that is to say, my Intimate, my Innermost, my Monad.

I cleaned China, and I also cleaned the Western World. The black magicians from China and from the Western World were as numerous as the sand of the sea.

All of the black magicians from China were depending upon the orders of the Black Lodge called the Black Dragon.

All of the black magicians from the Western World were depending upon a certain black magician from Rome.

Hence, millions of souls from the fatalities of the Second World War fell into the abyss.

The Lords of Karma established a tribunal within the Avitchi. Power was granted to me in order to judge these black magicians and also to execute their punishment.

This is how verse 11 from the nineteenth chapter of the Apocalypse was fulfilled. This verse states:

> *And I saw heaven opened, and behold a white horse; and he that sat upon him was called Faithful and True, and in righteousness he doth judge and make war.* REVELATION 19:11

We could fill enormous volumes if we would tell in detail all of the scenes and all of the things which I performed in order to clean the Earth from all evilness. If we had not done all of this, it would have been impossible to initiate the age of Aquarius.

I, Samael Aun Weor, am the Avatar of Aquarius; I am the Initiator of the New Age. I am faithfully accomplishing my mission. I profoundly thank the Masters for the honor which they granted to me.

The Masters placed over my head many brilliant crowns and my vesture seemed to be dipped in blood while in mid-battle.

This is how verses 12 and 13 of the nineteenth chapter of the Apocalypse were accomplished. They state:

> *His eyes were as a flame of fire, and on his head were many crowns; and he had a name written, that no man knew, but he himself.*

> *And he was clothed with a vesture dipped in blood; and his name is called The Word of God.* REVELATION 19:12-13

The name of my Real Being is hidden within the name "Word of God" because the Bible is highly symbolic.

God is represented with the monosyllable "Aun" or "Aum." Word or Verb is within "Weor," which is pronounced Veor, so the W is the V sound. This W together with the remaining three letters (e-r-o) of Verb and Word form "Weor." Thus, we have the name Aun Weor (Aum Weor, Aum Word, God Word) hidden within the phrase "Word of God."

My name was purposely hidden within the phrase "Word of God" because I have accomplished this mission with the lost word, with the Word of God, with the signed sentence that is within the luminous and spermatic Fiat of the first instant with the hiss of the Fohat.

This is how, after all of this, the Astral plane became clean of black magicians.

The lost word of the Black Lodge, "Mathrem," which appears within the monograph of ninth degree from the school of Sodom, protected them for millions of years within the veil of obscurity. Yet now in the Millennium, it will not protect them anymore.

The Gods judged the "Great Whore" (Humanity) with the number 6. Thus, they considered her unworthy. The sentence from the Gods was: *To the abyss! To the abyss! To the abyss!*

The Astral plane became clean as millions of human souls fell into the abyss. Yet, billions of demons remained within the physical plane with bodies of flesh and bones. This is when the Gods had to judge the Great Whore (Humanity) in order to cast her into the abyss.

The Third World War is already inevitable. People will die by the millions like the sand from the sea. This has to happen in order for verses 17 and 18 from the nineteenth chapter of the Apocalypse to be fulfilled. These verses state:

> *And I saw an angel standing in the sun; and he cried with a loud voice, saying to all the fowls that fly in midst of heaven, Come and gather yourselves together unto the supper of the great God.*

> *That ye may eat the flesh of kings, and the flesh of captains, and the flesh of mighty men, and flesh of horses, and of them that sit on them, and the flesh of all men, both free and bound, both small and great.* Revelation 19:17-18

Human beings will die by the millions, like the sand of the sea. The colossus from the north will pay its Karma. There will be war between the east and the west for the good of this humanity, thus said Jehovah of hosts. The demonic souls from the dead of the Third World War will sink into the abyss.

From the year 1950 henceforth, the souls who will receive physical bodies will be only those who will have the chance to be properly prepared to live in the age of Aquarius. Eventually, our planet will become almost barren; yet, millions of inhabitants from other planets will come in order to illuminate the age of Aquarius.

We spoke previously about "UFOs" in our first edition of the book *The Perfect Matrimony*. We explained in that book that they are flying ships, and that the instructors of Aquarius will come in them.

The demon souls of the human beings from our Earth are establishing themselves within the Avitchi (abyss) of the black moon. They have the same customs which they had when they were here. Thus, they have formed the same environment such as they had on our Earth.

The Hierarchs from the Black Lodge are obeyed by the billions of demon souls.

The fortunetelling tables, the famous magical figures of Phurbu over the squared turtle, the plates and tables for sacrifices, the circles of "Chinsreg" are seen everywhere in this new black habitat.

All of those black magicians have their Kundabuffer awakened (Kundalini awakened in the negative way). Therefore, they incessantly copulate in order to practice their black Sexual Magic with the goal of strengthening their Kundalini in the negative way.

We previously stated in this book that there are two types of Sexual Magic. One is a Sexual Magic that creates life and the other which creates death. The first one is White Magic and the second is black magic.

At first, these black magicians made thousands of experiments in order to escape from the Avitchi, yet all of their experiments failed.

They believed in the beginning that the Avitchi was a cave or something of the sort. Now they are finally realizing that the Avitchi is a plane from Nature which is similar to the physical environment of the Earth. This is because they made millions of experiments, they consulted their books, yet they did not have any success for all of their experiments failed.

They will remain there until the age of Capricorn, then afterwards, the last opportunity will be granted to them to repent of their evilness.

The fire transforms everything, because everything came out of the fire and everything returns into the fire.

The redemption of the human being is in the fire. Fohat transforms everything which is, everything which has been, and everything which will be.

We have defeated death; thus, we are immortal. The sword of Damocles threateningly rises against the mute skull. The world is within the fire of Alchemy; hence, all refuse is falling into the abyss.

I have finished this book in the middle of the tempest. The cannons are roaring, the Earth trembles, the terrible rumble of the thunder is heard, and within the frightful blowing of the hurricane, majestic voices and terrible words are heard.

The Earth is in flames and the Fohat is incessantly hissing. Thus, within the terrible hissing of the Fohat, the sentence of the Gods of Fire is heard:

To the abyss!

To the abyss!

To the abyss!

Hymn for the New Era
by the great Avatar of Aquarius (to be sung in chorus)

I

Let us break the chains...
tyranny has already fallen...
Om... om... om...
Life is in festivity..
let us break the chains...
om... om... om...

II

Good Jesus, come, come, come,
He does not want slaves.
Javhe has already fallen, Luzbel has already fallen.

III

Let us break the chains...
tyranny has already fallen...
Om... om... om...
Life is in festivity..
let us break the chains...

IV

In the infinite space,
within divine lightning,
the Gods immortal
sing with heavenly chanting...

V

The black night has already passed...
with its painful scaffolds...
now let us chant to the heroes of the night
a chant of love...

VI

Let us break the chains...
tyranny has already fallen...
Om... om... om...
Life is in festivity..
let us break the chains...
om... om... om...

VI

Good Jesus, come, come, come.
He does not want slaves.
Javhe has already fallen, Luzbel has already fallen.
now we are free,
now we are wise,
Luzbel has already fallen...

VIII

Let us break the chains...
tyranny has already fallen...
Om... om... om...
Life is in festivity..
let us break the chains...
om... om... om...
INRI INRI INRI

The best of Buddhism is within Gnosis, the best of the Egyptian, Chaldean,
Zoroastrian, etc. science is within Gnosis.

EPILOGUE
The Gnostic Institutions

The Gnostic Movement is the synthesis-movement for the new Age of Aquarius.

All of the seven schools of Yoga are within Gnosis, yet they are in a synthesized and absolutely practical way.

There is Tantric Hatha Yoga in the practices of the Maithuna (Sexual Magic). There is practical Raja Yoga in the work with the chakras. There is Jnana Yoga in our practices and mental disciplines which we have cultivated in secrecy for millions of years. We have Bhakti Yoga in our prayers and Rituals. We have Laya Yoga in our meditation and respiratory exercises. Samadhi exists in our practices with the Maithuna and during our deep meditations. We live the path of Karma Yoga in our upright actions, in our upright thoughts, in our upright feelings, etc.

The secret science of the Sufis and of the Whirling Dervishes is within Gnosis. The secret doctrine of Buddhism and of Taoism is within Gnosis. The sacred magic of the Nordics is within Gnosis. The wisdom of Hermes, Buddha, Confucius, Mohammed and Quetzalcoatl, etc., etc., is within Gnosis. Gnosis is the Doctrine of Christ.

Jesus of Nazareth is truly the man of synthesis. Jesus of Nazareth was an Essenian and he studied Hebraic wisdom. He had two masters (Rabbis) during his infancy. Nevertheless and furthermore, in spite of his profound knowledge of the Zohar, Talmud, and Torah, he is an Egyptian Initiate, an Egyptian Mason. Jesus of Nazareth studied within the pyramid of Kefren. He is an Egyptian Hierophant. He also traveled through Chaldea, Persia, Europe, India, and Tibet. The travels of Jesus were not tourist travels, they were travels for the purpose of studying.

Secret documents exist in Tibet which show that Jesus, the Great Gnostic Master was in Lhasa, the capital of Tibet, headquarters of the Dalai Lama.

Jesus visited the Cathedral of Jo Khang, the Holy Cathedral of Tibet. Tremendous was all of the knowledge that Jesus acquired in those countries and in all of those ancient schools of Mysteries...

The Great Master Jesus delivered in a synthesized way all the knowledge of Buddhism, Hermeticism, Zoroastrianism, the Talmud, Chaldea, Tibet, etc., which was already summarized in his Gnosis.

Jesus did not found the Roman Catholic Church, but Jesus founded the Gnostic Church. The Gnostic Church existed in the times of Saint Augustine. This is the Church which was known by Jeronimo, Empedocles, Saint Thomas, Marcion de Ponto, Clement of Alexandria, Tertulian, Saint Ambrosio, Harpocrates and all of the first Fathers of the Church. In that epoch, the Church was named the Catholic Gnostic Church.

The Roman Catholic Church in its present form was not founded by Jesus. This Roman Church is a deviation or corruption, a fallen branch of the holy Gnosticism. The Roman Catholic Church is a cadaver.

Humanity needs to return to the point of departure, it needs to return to the holy Gnosticism of the Hierophant Jesus. Humanity needs to return to the primeval Christianity, to the Gnostic Christianity.

The doctrine of Jesus Christ is the doctrine of the Essenes, the doctrine of the Nazarenes, Peratisens, or Peratas, etc.

The doctrine of Jesus Christ is condensed Yoga, essential Yoga, Tibetan Magic, Zen Buddhism, practical Buddhism, Hermetic Science, etc.

All ancient wisdom is within Gnosticism and it is already totally masticated and digested.

Therefore, Jesus, the Divine Master, is the Instructor of the World. If truly what we want is the realization of our Innermost Self, then let us practice Gnosis, let us live the path of the Gnostic Arhat.

The best exposition of the Secret Doctrine resides in the Gnostic synthesis of the great Hierophant Jesus the Christ.

Gnosis saves us work and study, for if we did not have the synthesis of Christ, we would need to bring into our heads millions of volumes and to travel around the entire world with the goal of finding the path.

Fortunately, already one Being did it and this Being was Jesus the Christ. He studied in the Buddhist Cathedral of Jo Khang, investigating very ancient Tibetan books.

Therefore, why do we need to do the same investigative work that he did? He already did that work. He delivered the whole of Yoga in a synthesized way, the whole of the Secret Science. So what else could we want?

Our duty is to study Gnosis and to live it; this is what is important. If they laugh at us, if they attack us, if they calumniate us, what does it matter to science or to us?

You can be sure, beloved reader, the best of Yoga is within Gnosis.

The best of Buddhism is within Gnosis, the best of the Egyptian, Chaldean, Zoroastrian, etc. science is within Gnosis. Therefore, what more? What more do we want? What more are we searching for?

The Gnostic Movement is the revolutionary movement for the new Aquarian Era. Yet, presently, many reactionary, extemporaneous and retarded individuals, who call themselves Gnostics, exist.

They excommunicate us because we divulge the Great Arcanum, the Maithuna; they say that we are doing a pansexualistic, sinful labor. They do not want humanity to receive the clue of the realization of the Innermost Self.

The Secretary of the Gnostic Institutions has received letters from one of those pseudo-Rosicrucians, pseudo-Gnostics, in which he affirms to be with Gnosis and with the Maithuna (Sexual Magic), yet he wants such a clue not to be delivered to this poor suffering humanity. Firstly, he says that people have to be prepared before receiving the knowledge of the Maithuna, etc. Nonetheless, such a sanctimonious leader, while addressing himself to certain students, contradicts himself. He talks against the Gnostic Movement and against the Great Arcanum, qualifying us as pornographic, etc.

Really, what he wants is not to allow others to enter onto the Path of the Razor's Edge. He is one of those who Jesus refers to when saying:

*Ye shut up the kingdom of heaven against men: for ye neither go
in yourselves, neither suffer ye them that are entering to go in.*
Matthew 23:13

He knows the clue of Sexual Magic; he knows the Maithuna, yet he does not want others to know it. He pledged himself to hide the Truth from the poor human beings.

Frankly, we have resolved to push ourselves to fight without quarrels, to fight to death in order to initiate the New Aquarian Age. It does not matter if they criticize us, if they insult us, if they betray us.

Gnosis must be delivered to humanity at any cost. Jesus taught Gnosis and we deliver it to humanity no matter what the cost might be.

The Gnostic Movement presents this Gnostic knowledge in a revolutionary way. The Gnostic Movement is one hundred percent revolutionary. The Gnostic Movement has been formed in order to initiate a new era which is directed by a revolutionary planet. This planet is Uranus, the planet of sexuality, the planet of the revolution on the march.

In these years of Aquarius, the Gnostic Movement must tremendously fight the good battle for the new Era of Aquarius.

Each Gnostic sanctuary must select a missionary. All missionaries must push themselves to battle to the death for the victory of Jesus the Christ.

All of the Gnostic lumisials must perform an intensive Gnostic expansion through pamphlets, circulars, brochures, books, radio broadcasts, newspapers, etc.

Whosoever wants Christification must be ready to give even the last drop of his blood for the Christ and for this suffering humanity.

The selfish ones, those who only think of themselves and only of their own progress, will never achieve the Christification.

Presently, the Gnostic Movement has more than four million people in the whole of America; yet, it needs to grow more; it needs to become powerful and gigantic, with the goal of transforming the world for the new era which we have already started.

Former years were terrible, since we were betrayed many times by villains. Yet, we conquered, we won the battle... Now we are more powerful, more strong, more numerous... Former years have ended with total victory for the Gnostic Movement.

The Era of Aquarius must be a war to the death against ignorance, fanaticism, and error. It is necessary to intensely work in the Great Work of the Father and to bring into our Gnostic columns thousands and thousands of people. We need to strengthen the worldwide Gnostic salvation army.

Remember, Gnostic brethren, that the practical synthesis of all the yogas, lodges, orders, religions, schools, systems, etc., is in the Gnosis of the Cosmic Christ.

Our great Master, Jesus the Christ, deeply studied Yoga in its entirety and the whole of the ancient wisdom. Then after, he delivered all of this, already digested and perfectly simplified in an absolutely practical way in his Gnosticism.

There is Gnosis in the Buddhist doctrine, in the Tantric Buddhism from Tibet, in the Zen Buddhism from Japan, in the Chan Buddhism of China, in Sufism, in the Whirling Dervishes, in the Egyptian, Persian, Chaldean, Pythagorean, Greek, Aztec, Mayan, Inca, etc., wisdom.

If we carefully study the Christian Gospels, we will find in them Pythagorean mathematics, the Chaldean and Babylonian parable, and the formidable Buddhist moral.

The system of teaching which was adopted by Jesus was the system of the Essenes. Certainly, the Essenes were one hundred percent Gnostics.

Therefore, the Four Gospels are Gnostic Gospels and they cannot be understood without the Maithuna (Sexual Magic).

It becomes absurd to adulterate Gnosis with different teachings, because the Christian Gospel prohibits adultery. It is absurd to conceive of Gnosis without the Maithuna.

We can drink the wine of Gnosis (Divine Wisdom) within a Greek, Buddhist, Sufi, Aztec, Egyptian, etc. cup, yet we must not adulterate this delicious wine with strange doctrines.

The practical synthesis of Gnosticism in its absolutely revolutionary way is taught within the Gnostic Institutions.

The Gnostic lumisials from the Gnostic Institutions are esoteric academies and temples of solar liturgy.

Really, the Gnostic rituals are solar liturgy. In this day and age, the human being still does not possess a Solar Body (Astral Body).

The Astral Body is a luxury which very few can give to themselves. The present human being, that is to say, the intellectual animal, possesses only a Lunar Body (Molecular Body).

Thus, the Intellectual Animal is a slave of the lunar influence. He carries the Moon within his molecular, phantom-like, negative, lunar body.

Really, the present human being is a hybrid mixture of plant and phantom.

The unique thing which the Intellectual Animal carries within his lunar body is the legion of "I's" and the sleeping Buddhata.

This is why the Gnostic Institutions teach the Maithuna, because with it the human being can build the Solar Body.

It is necessary for the human being to be liberated from the Moon and to be converted into a Solar Spirit.

The Gnostic rituals connect us with the solar force. It is necessary to fight against the lunar force to become truly free. This is what the Gnostic Institutions want.

The Sun is life in abundance, yet the Moon is death; the Moon is materialism, drunkenness, banquets, lust, anger, greed, envy, pride, laziness, disbelief, etc.

The Sun is fire, wisdom, love, divine Spirit, splendor, etc.

The Sun is the Cosmic Christ, the Verb, the Great Word. The Four Gnostic Gospels constitute the Solar Drama, the Drama of Christ.

We need to live the Solar Drama; we need to convert ourselves into the central personage of that Cosmic Drama.

It does not matter if they criticize us, if they abhor us, if they hate us because we are divulging the Maithuna (Sexual Magic) for the good of this poor failed humanity.

The degenerated infrasexuals will never forgive the fact that we defend suprasexuality.

Really, it causes pain to see those poor infrasexuals in the Molecular World (Astral Plane) after death. Their lunar bodies convert them into lunar women who wander throughout the Molecular World as somnambulists, asleep, cold, and unconscious creatures.

What was the good of all of the subjective practices of these infrasexuals? What was the good of all of their beliefs, systems, orders, etc.? To no avail, the infrasexuals will try to gain their liberation by despising sex, by renouncing the Maithuna (Sexual Magic), by abstinence, by abuse, or by following the degenerated path of the homosexuals and masturbators, etc.

Uselessly, the mistaken, sincere ones try to create the Solar Bodies by practicing respiratory exercises, yoga without Maithuna, or similar exercises, or with vegetarian diets, etc.

It is completely demonstrated that we are children of sex and that only through sex can we create.

Really, we can only create the Solar Bodies with sex. We can convert ourselves into Solar Spirits only with the marvelous force of the Third Logos.

We want to teach the Solar Religion to this humanity. We want to deliver to these poor lunar phantoms the Solar Doctrine of the Cosmic Christ, with only one unique goal, which is the Christification of the human being.

It is urgent for the Christ to be born within the heart of the human being. It is necessary for each human being to be converted into a Solar Angel.

The Gnostic Institutions (Gnostic Movement) have a gigantic task in the Era of Aquarius which we are starting. The sacred mission of teaching the Doctrine of the Solar Logos to this poor humanity has been granted to us.

We must fight until death in order to make the Gnostic Movement each time more and more powerful. We need this Movement to become omnipotent for the good of the many millions of human beings which are heading towards the path of the Second Death.

We need to be compassionate and to deliver the Solar Doctrine to this humanity, no matter what the cost might be.

Glossary

For more terms, visit www.gnosticteachings.org

Agrippa, Heinrich Cornelius: (1486-1535) A writer of renaissance esoterica. "In order to cease being a psychological robot, it becomes necessary to dominate oneself. Faust achieved it, but Cornelius Agrippa did not achieve it because he just chose to theorize." - *The Revolution of the Dialectic*

Besant, Annie: (1847-1933) English social reformer and theosophist. She crusaded for free thought, birth control, and women's rights. After her conversion (1889) to Theosophy — a philosophical, religious movement founded by Blavatsky (below) — Besant went to India, where she spent the rest of her life. She founded the Central Hindu College at Varanasi and was politically active. For many years, beginning in 1916, she campaigned for Indian home rule. She also traveled extensively in Great Britain and the United States with Krishnamurti, her adopted son whom she presented as a new messiah, a claim he later renounced (See *Endocrinology and Criminology* by Samael Aun Weor). Besant wrote widely on theosophy and was president of the Theosophical Society from 1907 until her death.

Blavatsky, Helena Petrovna: Quoted from the Theosophical Online Library: "HPB was born in Russia. She spent her early years in travel, arriving in New York in 1873. Together with Colonel Henry Steele Olcott, William Q. Judge and others, she formed the Theosophical Society. She published her first book, *Isis Unveiled,* in 1877. The following year HPB and Olcott went to India to establish the TS there, leaving Judge to continue the work in the United States. HPB edited the magazine *The Theosophist* while in India. She moved on to England in 1887 and established the Blavatsky Lodge in London. She also started a magazine, *Lucifer* (from the Latin "Luciferus", meaning the Light-bringer, the Morning Star). HPB's master-work, *The Secret Doctrine,* was published in 1888. HPB suffered from a chronic kidney disease for many years. She contracted the flu and died on May 8, 1891." She wrote in her *Secret Doctrine,* "In Century the Twentieth some disciple more informed, and far better fitted, may be sent by the Masters of Wisdom to give final and irrefutable proofs that there exists a Science called Gupta-Vidya; and that, like the once-mysterious sources of the Nile, the source of all religions and philosophies now known to the world has been for many ages forgotten and lost to men, but is at last found." This prediction is a reference to Samael Aun Weor.

Bodhisattva: (Sanskrit) Literally, Bodhi means "enlightenment" or "wisdom." Sattva means "essence" or "goodness," therefore the term Bodhisattva literally means "essence of wisdom." In the esoteric or secret teachings of Tibet and Gnosticism, a Bodhisattva is a human being who has reached the Fifth Initiation of Fire (Tiphereth) and has chosen to continue working by means of the Straight Path, renouncing the easier Spiral Path (in Nirvana), and returning instead to help suffering humanity. By means of this sacrifice, this individual incarnates the Christ (Avalokitesvara), thereby embodying the supreme source of wisdom and compassion. This is the entrance to the Direct Path to complete liberation from the ego, a route that only very few take, due to the fact that one must pay the entirety of one's karma in one life. Those who have taken this road have been the most remarkable figures in human history: Jesus, Buddha, Mohammed, Krishna, Moses, Padmasambhava, Milarepa, Joan of Arc, Fu-Ji, and many others whose names are not remembered or known. Of course, even among bodhisattvas there are many levels of Being: to be a bodhisattva does not mean that one is enlightened. Interestingly, the Christ in Hebrew is called Chokmah, which means "wisdom," and in Sanskrit the same is Vishnu, the root of the word "wisdom." It is Vishnu who sent his Avatars into the world in order to guide humanity. These avatars were Krishna, Buddha, Rama, and the Avatar of this age: the Avatar Kalki. "The truly humble Bodhisattva never praises himself. The humble Bodhisattva says, 'I am just a miserable slug from the mud of the earth, I am a nobody. My person has no value. The work is what is worthy.' The Bodhisattva is the human soul of a Master. The Master is the internal God." - *The Aquarian Message*

Bons: (or Bhons) The oldest religion in Tibet. It was largely overshadowed (some say persecuted) by the arrival of Buddhism. Samael Aun Weor had accepted the statements of earlier investigators which described the Bon religion as essentially Black; but upon further investigation he discovered that they are not necessarily Black, just extreme in some practices.

Cagliostro: "Cagliostro was a disciple of Count Saint Germain. Cagliostro was an alchemist; he transmuted the lead into gold and made genuine diamonds. This Master was known in the distinct places of the world, under different names in different countries. He was known with the following names: Tis-chio, Milissa, Belonte, D'anna, Fenix, Pellegrini, Balsamo, Mesmer, Harut and Cagliostro.

This famous historical lineage was recorded by Alexandre Dumas in his work entitled, *The Queens Necklace.* Cagliostro had many Alchemist disciples in Strasbourg. He was judged and persecuted by the Inquisition, sent into the bastille and later into the fortress of Leone. The Inquisition condemned him to death, but the enigmatic and powerful Count Cagliostro mysteriously disappeared from the prison. Death could not do anything to Cagliostro." from *The Aquarian Message*

Drukpas: A large sect which broke from the Kagyug-pa "the Ones of the Oral Tradition." They considered themselves as the heirs of the Indian Gurus: their Teaching, which goes back to Vajradhara, was conveyed through Dakini, from Naropa to Marpa and then to the ascetic and mystic poet Milarepa. Later on, Milarepa's disciples founded new monasteries, and new threads appeared, among which are the Karmapa and the Brugpa (also called Dugpa or Dad Dugpa). All those schools form the Kagyug-pa order, in spite of episodic internal quarrels and extreme differences in practice. The Dag Dugpa sect is recognized by their ceremonial large red hats. They have established a particular worship of the Dorje (Vajra, or thunderbolt, a symbol of the phallus), which descended from heaven and fell upon the earth at Séra in Eastern Tibet. Samael Aun Weor wrote repeatedly in many books that the Dag Dugpas practice and teach Black Tantrism.

Damocles: According to classical mythology, Damocles so persistently praised the power and happiness of Dionysius that the tyrant, in order to show the precariousness of rank and power, gave a banquet and had a sword suspended above the head of Damocles by a single hair. Hence the expression "the sword of Damocles" to mean an ever-present peril.

Demosthenes: (384–322 B.C.) A Greek lawyer who overcame a weak voice to become widely considered the greatest Greek political orator.

Eye of Dangma: Dangma is a Sanskrit term for "a purified soul," thus the Eye of Dangma is a reference to the spiritual sight of the elevated Initiate. It is polyvoyance, the capacity to perceive all the dimensions of nature, and is rooted in the pineal gland. From Blavatsky's *The Secret Doctrine:* "In India it is called 'The Eye of Siva,' but beyond the great range it is known as 'Dangma's opened eye' in esoteric phraseology. Dangma means 'a purified soul,' one who has become a Jivanmukta, the highest adept, or rather a Mahatma. His 'opened eye' is the inner spiritual eye of the seer, and the faculty which manifests through it is not clairvoyance as ordinarily understood, i.e., the power of seeing at a distance, but rather the faculty of spiritual intuition, through which direct and certain knowledge is obtainable. This faculty is intimately connected with the 'third eye,' which mythological tradition ascribes to certain races of men."

Heindel, Max: (b. Carl Louis von Grasshoff) was born in Copenhagen, Denmark July 23, 1865. At the age of sixteen years he left home to learn the engineering profession. For a number of years he was Chief Engineer on one of the large passenger steamers of the Cunard Line plying between America and Europe. From 1895 to 1901, he was a consulting engineer in New York city. Max Heindel moved to Los Angeles, California, in 1903. He became interested in the study of metaphysics and joined the Theosophical Society of Los Angeles, of which he was Vice-President in 1904 and 1905. In 1907 he travelled to Germany with his friend Dr. Alma Von Brandis to hear a cycle of lectures by Rudolf Steiner. Heindel returned to America in the spring of 1909 where he at once started to formulate the Rosicrucian teachings, published as a book entitled *The Rosicrucian Cosmo-Conception*, a work of mystical and occult science (Esoteric Christianity). It contains a comprehensive outline of the evolutionary processes of man and the universe, correlating science with religion. Following the foundation of The Rosicrucian Fellowship at Oceanside, CA in 1909 he started, with the aid of his wife Augusta Foss Heindel the task of distributing and disseminating the Rosicrucian teachings. From 1909 to 1919, suffering a severe heart condition and with an adverse financial situation, Max Heindel was able to perform a valuable work for the brothers of the Rose Cross: he left a legacy of books, lectures and lessons which are translated into many languages all over the world. He died in Oceanside, California on January 6, 1919.

Human Being: According to Gnostic Anthropology, a true Human Being is an individual who has conquered the animal nature within and has thus created the Soul, the Mercabah of the Kabbalists, the Sahu of the Egyptians, the To Soma Heliakon of the Greeks: this is "the Body of Gold of the Solar Man." A true Human Being is one with the Monad, the Inner Spirit. A true Human Being has reconquered the innocence and perfection of Eden, and has become what Adam was intended to be: a King of Nature, having power over Nature. The Intellectual Animal, however, is controlled by nature, and thus is not a true Human Being. Examples of true Human Beings are all those great saints of all ages and cultures: Jesus, Moses, Mohammed, Krishna, and many others whose names were never known by the public.

Iamblicus: (c. A.D. 250-325) Among the most important of the
Neoplatonic philosophers. He was a student of Plotinus' disciple
Porphyry. His influential treatise *On the Mysteries of Egypt* expresses
High Magic, which operates through the agency of the gods.
Agrippa refers frequently to Iamblichus in his *Occulta Philosophia.*
Iamblicus wrote, "They (the Beings we invoke) will not hearken
to the person who is invoking them if he is not pure from sexual
contamination..." And, "Theurgy unites us more strongly with
divine nature. This nature is engendered by itself and acts in
accordance with its own powers. It is intelligent and sustains
everything; it is the ornament of the universe and invites us to the
intelligent truth, to perfection, and to share this perfection with
others. It unites us so intimately to all the creative acts of the Gods
in proportion to the capacity of each one of us. After accomplishing
these sacred rites, the soul is consolidated within the actions of the
intelligence of the Gods until identifying itself with them. Thus it is
absorbed by the primeval and divine Essence. Such is the object of
the sacred initiations of the Egyptians."

Intellectual Animal: When the Intelligent Principle, the Monad, sends
its spark of consciousness into Nature, that spark, the *anima*, enters
into manifestation as a simple mineral. Gradually, over millions
of years, the anima gathers experience and evolves up the chain
of life until it perfects itself in the level of the mineral kingdom.
It then graduates into the plant kingdom, and subsequently into
the animal kingdom. With each ascension the spark receives
new capacities and higher grades of complexity. In the animal
kingdom it learns procreation by ejaculation. When that animal
intelligence enters into the human kingdom, it receives a new
capacity: reasoning, the intellect; it is now an anima with intellect:
an Intellectual Animal. That spark must then perfect itself in the
human kingdom in order to become a complete and perfect Human
Being, an entity that has conquered and transcended everything
that belongs to the lower kingdoms. Unfortunately, very few
Intellectual Animals perfect themselves; most remain enslaved by
their animal nature, and thus are reabsorbed by Nature, a process
belonging to the Devolving side of life and called by all the great
religions Hell or the Second Death.

Innermost: the Intimate, Atman, the Spirit, Chesed, our individual
divine Father. "The Innermost is the ardent flame of Horeb. In
accordance with Moses, the Innermost is the Ruach Elohim who
sowed the waters in the beginning of the world. He is the Sun King,
our Divine Monad, the Alter-Ego of Cicerone. - *The Revolution of
Beelzebub*

Kingdoms of Nature: All the monadic sparks which evolve and devolve through the mechanical cycles of nature pass through four kingdoms in ascendant and descendant order, within the mineral, plant, animal and intellectual animal (humanoid) kingdoms. Only those who perform the Great Work of the realization of the Being escape this Wheel of Samsara, to enter into Conscious Evolution within the Superior Kingdoms.

Leadbeater, C.W.: A writer of Theosophical Occultism famous for such books as *The Elementals* and *The Chakras.*

Logos: (Greek) means Verb or Word. In Greek and Hebrew metaphysics, the unifying principle of the world. The Logos is the manifested deity of every nation and people; the outward expression or the effect of the cause which is ever concealed. (Speech is the "logos" of thought). The Logos has three aspects, known universally as the Trinity or Trimurti. The First Logos is the Father, Brahma. The Second Logos is the Son, Vishnu. The Third Logos is the Holy Spirit, Shiva. One who incarnates the Logos becomes a Logos. "The Logos is not an individual. The Logos is an army of ineffable beings." - *Endocrinology & Criminology*

Lully, Raymond: (b. 1232) Catalan philosopher, b. Palma, Majorca. Of a wealthy family, he lived in ease until c.1263, when he had a religious experience and was fired with ambition to convert Muslims to Christianity. He studied Arabic language and literature and founded (1276) a college in Majorca for the study of Arabic. In 1292 he went to Tunis and challenged Muslim scholars to public debates. He was forcibly deported but made a second trip to North Africa in 1307 to combat the teachings of Averroës and again was banished. The tradition that he was stoned to death on a third trip that began in 1315 cannot be substantiated. Lully's chief work—*Ars magna* [the great art]—was a defense of Christianity against the teachings of Averroës. Lully maintained that philosophy (including science) was not divorced from theology and that every article of faith could be demonstrated perfectly by logic.

Lumisial: "A place of light." A Gnostic Lumisial is a generator of spiritual energy, a Gnostic school which maintains the ancient initiatic Three Chamber structure. The source of power is the Cosmic Christ, and the means to receive and transform it are within the Second and Third Chambers. "We are therefore working, my dear brethren, to initiate the Era of Aquarius. We are working in order to save what is possible, meaning, those who allow themselves to be saved. This is why it is necessary that we shape our Gnostic Movements and that we organize them each time better; that we

establish the Three Chambers. Our Gnostic Movements must have exactly Three Chambers. Each Lumisial must have Three Chambers for the instruction of our students. Our Gnostic Centers receive a name in a very pure language that flows like a river of gold that runs under the thick jungle of the sun; that name is LUMISIALS."
- *The Final Catastrophe and the Extraterrestrials*

Manteia: A term from the Eleusian Mysteries referring to a state of consciousness in which the essence becomes free of the ego.

Master: Like many terms related to spirituality, this one is grossly misunderstood. Samael Aun Weor writes while describing the Germanic *Edda*, "In this Genesis of creation we discover Sexual Alchemy. The Fire fecundated the cold waters of chaos. The masculine principle Alfadur fecundated the feminine principle Niffleheim, dominated by Surtur [the Darkness], to bring forth life. That is how Ymir is born, the father of the giants, the Internal God of every human being, the Master." Therefore, the Master is the Innermost, Atman, the Father. "The value of the human person which is the intellectual animal called human being is less than the ash of a cigarette. However, the fools feel themselves to be giants. Unfortunately, within all the pseudo-esoteric currents a great amount of mythomaniac people exist, individuals who feel themselves to be Masters, people who enjoy when others call them Masters, individuals who believe themselves to be Gods, individuals who presume to be Saints. The only one who is truly great is the Spirit, the Innermost. We, the intellectual animals, are leaves that the wind tosses about... No student of occultism is a Master. True Masters are only those who have reached the Fifth Initiation of Major Mysteries. Before the Fifth Initiation nobody is a Master."
- Excerpts from *The Perfect Matrimony* "You are not the Master, you are only the sinning shadow of He who has never sinned. Remember that only your internal Lamb is the Master. Remember that even though your internal God is a Hierarch of fire, you, poor slug, are only a human being and as a human being you will always be judged. Your internal Lamb could be a planetary God, but you, poor slug of the mud, do not forget, always remember that you are only the shadow of your God. Poor sinning shadow..! Do not say "I am this God" or "I am that Master," because you are only a shadow that must resolve to die and be slaughtered in order not to serve as an obstacle for your internal God. It is necessary for you to reach supreme humbleness." - from *The Aquarian Message*.

Mesmer, Franz Anton: (1734–1815) German physician. He studied in Vienna. His interest in "animal magnetism" developed into a system

of treatment through hypnotism that was called mesmerism. An unsympathetic medical and scientific community caused him to be expelled first from Vienna, and in 1778 from Paris. He retired to his native Austria and to obscurity. "Mesmer was a marvelous man. He had a premonition that a double consciousness existed in human beings, thus he resolved to study it. He realized that a false consciousness exists as well as a real legitimate consciousness stored in our depths and that we underestimate the real legitimate consciousness. Therefore, Mesmer began to carry out experiments of magnetism which were, without a doubt, contrary to Hypnology."
- *The Revolution of the Dialectic*

Monad: (Latin) From monas, "unity; a unit, monad." "[The number] one is the Monad, the Unity, Iod-Heve or Jehovah, the Father who is in secret. It is the Divine Triad that is not incarnated within a Master who has not killed the ego. He is Osiris, the same God, the Word." - *Tarot and Kabbalah* "When spoken of, the Monad is referred to as Osiris. He is the one that has to Self-realize Himself... Our own particular Monad needs us and we need it. Once, while speaking with my Monad, my Monad told me, 'I am self-realizing Thee; what I am doing, I am doing for Thee.' Otherwise, why are we living? The Monad wants to Self-realize and that is why we are here. This is our objective." - *Tarot and Kabbalah*

Pleroma: (Greek) "Fullness," an ancient Gnostic term adopted to signify the divine world or Universal Soul. Space, developed and divided into a series of aeons. The abode of the invisible Gods. In correspondence to the Kabbalah, Pleroma refers to the World of Atziluth.

Prometheus: From Greek mythology, the son of the Titan Iapetus and of Clymene or Themis. Because he foresaw the defeat of the Titans by the Olympians, he sided with Zeus and thus was spared the punishment of the other Titans. According to one legend Prometheus created mankind out of clay and water. When Zeus mistreated man, Prometheus stole fire from the gods, gave it to man, and taught him many useful arts and sciences. In another legend he saved the human race from extinction by warning his son, Deucalion, of a great flood. This sympathy with mankind roused the anger of Zeus, who then plagued man with Pandora and her box of evils and chained Prometheus to a mountain peak in the Caucasus. In some myths he was released by Hercules; in others Zeus restored his freedom when Prometheus revealed the danger of Zeus' marrying Thetis, fated to bear a son who would be more powerful than his father.

Sahaja Maithuna: (Sanskrit) Sahaja, "natural." Maithuna, "sacramental intercourse"

Sodom: In the Bible, the principal of the Cities of the Plain (the others being Gomorrah, Admah, Zeboiim, and Zoar, which was spared) destroyed by fire from heaven because of their wickedness. Modern scholars believe that the cities were probably located near the S portion of the Dead Sea. The ruins at Bab edh-Dhra and Numeira have been identified by some with Sodom and Gomorrah, respectively.

Soma: This term has a variety of applications and two primary derviations: First, it is the name of the sacred drink of the Gods according to ancient Indian religious texts. The word soma means "to press," and refers to a drink made of the juice of a plant. This drink is related to the god Chandra "the bright," who is related to the Moon. (Chandra is often mistakenly called Soma). It was said that it was the force of Chandra the Moon that gave life to all animals, Gods, humans and spirits. (This is very interesting to consider in light of what Samael Aun Weor taught regarding the Selenite humanity, which inhabited the Moon in the previous Age). The second primary derivation is from the Greek, in which soma means "body." This word refers to the body and mind as one, and is the root of many terms, such as "psycho-soma-tic." In the context of the teachings of Samael Aun Weor, soma also refers to the moon and is a symbol of the woman. In modern times, the term is used to refer to hallucenogenic substances. "He to whom heaven and earth bow down; he at whose might the mountains are appalled; he who is the drinker of the Soma juice, the firm of frame, the adamant armed, the wielder of the thunderbolt; he, men, is Indra." - *Rig Veda*

Steiner, Dr. Rudolf: (1861-1925) Rudolf Steiner was born in the part of the Austro-Hungarian Empire that is modern day Croatia to a German-speaking middle-class family. In childhood he showed great precocity, teaching himself geometry at the age of eight and absorbing the fundamentals of philosophy, geography, calculus, Latin and Greek by the age of 15. Steiner took a degree in physics, chemistry and mathematics while simultaneously attending lectures in literature and philosophy at the University of Vienna. In addition to his interest in scientific and philosophical knowledge, Steiner also "complained" of being clairvoyant from early childhood, and by his early twenties had begun to develop his own philosophy of spiritual science, in which he sought to present a scientific, empirical approach to metaphysical considerations. Influenced by the spiritual writings of Goethe, the first of numerous publications on a variety of topics now appeared – *Truth and Knowledge, The Philosophy of Freedom, Goethe's Conception of the World* – texts which were to form the basis of Steiner's later influential work in education, medicine, agriculture and social science. Steiner went on to conduct hundreds of public and private lectures on diverse topics all over Europe. A large number of these lectures were transcribed and published. His multi-faceted genius has led to innovative and holistic approaches in medicine, science, education (Waldorf schools), special education, philosophy, religion, economics, agriculture (Bio-Dynamic method), architecture, drama, the new art of eurythmy, and other fields. In 1925 he founded the General Anthroposophical Society, which today has branches throughout the world.

Tsong Khapa: (1357-1419) founder of the Gelug school of Tibetan Buddhism and the First Dalai Lama. "In 1387, with just reason, the Tibetan reformer Tsong-Kahpa cast every book of Necromancy that he found into flames. As a result, some discontent Lamas formed an alliance with the aboriginal Bhons, and today they form a powerful sect of black magic in the regions of Sikkim, Bhutan and Nepal, submitting themselves to the most abominable black rites." - *The Revolution of Beelzebub* "Let us remember Tsong Khapa who reincarnated in Tibet; he was the Buddha Gautama previously." - from *Mental Representations*. Tsong Khapa said, "A female companion is the basis of accomplishment of liberation."

Urania: (Greek: Ourania) One of the nine Muses of Greek Mythology. Urania is related to astronomy or to the celestial realms, the heavens.

Vesta: (Roman name; known in Greek as Hestia) Hestia is the gentle, virgin goddess of the hearth-fire (both private & municipal), the home and family. She voluntarily relinquished her position as one of the twelve Olympians in place of Dionysos. As recompense she was made goddess of the sacrificial flame and granted a portion of all sacrifices to the gods. She is clearly a symbol of the the Divine Mother Kundalini, the root fire of all that exists. She was highly honored in every household from early times to the beginning of Christianity, when her worship was outlawed. Her public cult maintained a sacred building in which her priestesses, the vestal virgins, tended the communal hearth and fire, which was never allowed to die out. "To Hestia, fumigation from Aromatics. Daughter of Kronos, venerable dame, who dwellest amidst great fire's eternal flame; in sacred rites these ministers are thine, mystics much blessed, holy and divine. In thee the Gods have fixed their dwelling place, strong, stable basis of the mortal race. Eternal, much formed, ever florid queen, laughing and blessed, and of lovely mien; accept these rites, accord each just desire, and gentle health and needful good inspire." – *Orphic Hymn 84 to Hestia*

Vestal: A term derived from Roman religion, referring to a priestess of Vesta. While still little girls, they were chosen from prominent Roman families. Their duties included the preparation of sacrifices and the tending of the sacred fire. If any vestal broke her vow of chastity, she was entombed alive. The vestals had great influence in the Roman state. Their primary duty was to work in the sacred practice of Alchemy with the Initiates of the temple. The use of Vestals is no longer lawful and is not a part of any White Tradition in these times.

Index

Symbols

13th black initiation 35, 120
1950 73, 143, 149
3 34
311,040,000,000,000 years 5
33 canyons 34
33rd degree 34
33 years 34
6 149
777 83, 84

A

A.M.O.R.C. 17, 26
Abbadon 17, 67
Absolute 5, 28, 126, 129, 140
Abstinence 103, 161
Abstract Mind 44, 53
Abuse 161
Abyss 1, 2, 7, 11, 17, 26, 28, 29, 36, 37, 59,
    67, 68, 73, 84, 126, 131, 144, 145, 146,
    147, 149, 151
Accumulation 46, 61
Acolyte 61
Adam 109
Aditi 4
Adonai 146
Adultery 159
Adversities 85
age of Brahma ix
Age of Capricorn 150
Age of Gold 69
Agion tetra-gram 123
Agrippa, Cornelius 7, 163
Ain Soph 5
Air 4, 52, 67, 83, 84, 85, 86, 97, 105, 111,
    113
Air, ordeal of 84, 137
Akashic Records 3, 130, 131
Alaya 3
Alchemist 9, 18, 21, 33, 53
Alchemists 106
Alchemy 151, 169, 173, 190
Aloe 112, 113
Altruism 85
America 36, 92, 100, 122, 158
Amsha-Spentas 3
Amulet 92
Anagaric-hood 87
Anagarikas 17, 163
Anatomy 103, 135
Andrameleck 28

Angel 109, 132, 161
Angela 27
Angels 4, 13, 18, 31, 33, 35, 52, 55, 62, 64,
    67, 73, 77, 116, 137, 140
Anger 82, 130, 160
Animal "I" 17
Animal mind 45
Animal passion 17
Animals 52
Animal species 69
Animes 92
Antia rara ra ra.. 119
Antithesis 45
Anxieties 45
Apocalypse 4, 33, 63, 64, 65, 66, 144, 145,
    147, 148, 149
Apollyon 67
Aquarian Age 158
Aquarian Era 157
Aquarius 1, 143, 144, 145, 148, 149, 152,
    155, 158, 159, 161
Arahats 66
Arcadia 13, 14, 20, 29, 31, 69, 70, 71, 73,
    128, 129
Arcanum 24, 107, 118, 157
Archangels 40, 52, 57
Arco 35
Arhuacos Indians 92
Ariman 74, 89, 146
Aristotle 95
Ark 18, 30, 95
Ark of Alliance 95
Arrogant 110, 117
Aryan Root Race 52, 69, 95
Asia 146
Asleep 71, 100, 161
Assyria 107
Astaroth 39, 143
Astral 33, 81, 111, 112, 124
Astral body 14, 26, 52, 53, 59, 78, 96, 97,
    110, 122, 123, 124, 125, 129, 137, 160
Astral Light 18, 35, 53, 69, 113, 147
Astral plane 27, 38, 83, 84, 87, 98, 99, 100,
    110, 119, 120, 121, 122, 123, 124, 125,
    126, 127, 133, 134, 135, 143, 148, 149,
    161
Astral world 124, 134, 135
Astro 36
Asuncion 82
Atlantean 36, 71, 89, 92, 116

Books by the Same Author

Aquarian Message
Aztec Christic Magic
Book of the Dead
Book of the Virgin of Carmen
Buddha's Necklace
Christ Will
Christmas Messages (various)
Cosmic Ships
Cosmic Teachings of a Lama
Didactic Self-Knowledge
Dream Yoga (collected writings)
Elimination of Satan's Tail
Esoteric Course of Runic Magic
Esoteric Treatise of Hermetic Astrology
Esoteric Treatise of Theurgy
Fundamental Education
Fundamental Notions of Endocrinology
Gnostic Anthropology
Gnostic Catechism
The Great Rebellion
Greater Mysteries
Igneous Rose
The Initiatic Path in the Arcana of Tarot
    and Kabbalah

Introduction to Gnosis
Kabbalah of the Mayan Mysteries
Lamasery Exercises
Logos Mantra Theurgy
Manual of Practical Magic
Mysteries of Fire: Kundalini Yoga
Mystery of the Golden Blossom
Occult Medicine & Practical Magic
Parsifal Unveiled
The Perfect Matrimony
Pistis Sophia Unveiled
Revolution of Beelzebub
Revolution of the Dialectic
Revolutionary Psychology
Secret Doctrine of Anahuac
Three Mountains
Transmutation of Sexual Energy
Treatise of Sexual Alchemy
Yellow Book
Yes, There is Hell, a Devil, and Karma
Zodiacal Course
150 Answers from Master Samael Aun Weor

To learn more about Gnosis, visit gnosticteachings.org.

Thelema Press is a non-profit publisher dedicated to spreading the sacred universal doctrine to suffering humanity. All of our works are made possible by the kindness and generosity of sponsors. If you would like to make a tax-deductible donation, you may send it to the address below, or visit our website for other alternatives. If you would like to sponsor the publication of a book, please contact us at 212-501-6106 or help@gnosticteachings.org.

Thelema Press
PMB 192, 18645 SW Farmington Rd., Aloha OR 97007 USA
Phone: 212-501-6106 · Fax: 212-501-1676

Visit us online at:
gnosticteachings.org
gnosticradio.org
gnosticschool.org
gnosticstore.org
gnosticvideos.org